COGNITION

IN

EARLY CHILDHOOD

by

Janie Dyson Osborn
D. Keith Osborn

EDUCATION ASSOCIATES
Athens, Georgia

Cover Design: Jeanette M. Tuttle.
Illustrations for the Tasks: Janet Harkins.
Line drawings: Janet Harkins & Jeanette Tuttle.
Cover photo by the authors.
Child in cover photo: Kerry Wood

Send mail orders to:
Education Associates . . . Box 8021 . . . Athens, GA 30603

ISBN #: Cloth Edition: 0-918772-11-7
    Paper Edition: 0-918772-12-5
    Library of Congress Catalog Card
    Number: LC 83-071727

ii

We lovingly dedicate this book to
the memory of

D. A. Osborn.

PREFACE

This book has two major purposes: One, to help early childhood educators in their understanding of the cognitive growth and development of young children in the preschool and primary grades. Second, to provide the teacher with a group of cognitive tasks which will give added insight into the level and role of cognitive functioning.

These tasks are primarily derived from the work of Jean Piaget and his associates. As you will discover, the writers believe the tasks provide the teacher with an accurate picture into the ways children think and form the "roots" of their cognitive functioning. The reader may well ask, "Why not just give the child an IQ test and let it go at that? At least I would have an IQ score!" We feel that an IQ score *per se,* is of little value to the teacher. If she is equipped with the knowledge that Allison has an IQ of 98 and Robert has an IQ of 103, she actually has no firm knowledge from which to launch a program which will be beneficial to either Allison or Robert. We agree with Kohlberg and Maier (1973, p.489) that Piagetian measures "provide a rational standard for education intervention where psychometric intelligence tests do not."

As DeVries (1974, p. 747) has pointed out, IQ tests are not based on any theory of intelligence; whereas Piaget's tasks are derived from a research based theory.

"The theory accounts for changes in terms of gradual development of basic cognitive structure. Piagetian tasks are concerned with how the individual views and reasons about reality . . . Each task has theoretical significance and in itself reveals something about the individual's general development of his intelligence."

Piaget's tasks present the child with ambiguities of reality and ask the child to impose his ideas on these equivocal situations. The tasks, then, focus on the reasoning behind the child's conclusions.

We are not suggesting the abolition of IQ tests, but rather affirm the belief that more useful information is gained by the teacher through these task situations. McCelland (1973) has suggested that intelligence tests mainly predict test-taking and symbol-manipulation competencies. We feel that using these tasks will help the teacher see how the child thinks and provide insights for future program planning at both the individual and group level.

The authors wish to thank Ms. Sue Miller, a first grade school teacher in Valdosta, Georgia, for her contribution to the section on language. We also wish to acknowledge the help of Janet Harkins and Jeanette Tuttle for their illustrations of the cognitive tasks and the many line drawings throughout the book. One final word. In order to ease reading of the text, we have referred to the teacher as "she" and to the child as "he."

Janie Dyson Osborn
D. Keith Osborn

September 1983

Table of Contents

*Promoting Language Development written by Ms. Sue Miller.

CHAPTER ONE

Introduction to Cognitive Development

Introduction.

Throughout history there have been a wide variety of views concerning young children. The historical evidence suggests that in the early years of preliterate civilization, children were generally nurtured — but, by and large, left to their own devices for survival. There is very little evidence that a program of organized education was provided. It seems likely that primitive children learned the tasks of adulthood through observation or by modeling.

With the establishment of early cities, and more complex cultures, children were often viewed as "undesirable." During this pre-Christian period (about 2500 BC), children had little intrinsic value. Generally pagan religions did not value human life nor did these religions include the concept of a soul. The net result was that urban societies often viewed children as nonentities which permitted the practice of infanticide and child abuse.

Early Greek and Roman philosophers presented points of view concerning children and society which, in many ways, have affected our own contemporary approaches to the understanding and study of young children. From these early philosophical origins, two major points of view have emerged: Society's needs and the needs of the individual. These major philosophical views have had a profound effect upon the way we perceive children, their roles and our methods of rearing them. Let us briefly examine these two points of view.

1. **The needs of society.** Aristotle, Plato, and later John Locke, examined the basic needs of society in terms of community structure and individual function. Theorists of

another era who would agree with this approach, emphasized the concept of behaviorism. In the early part of this century, psychologists like Thorndike and Watson emphasized the philosophical ideas of behaviorism. They believed that the mind was a network of predictable responses to specific stimuli.

More recently psychologists like Hull and Skinner refined this theoretical approach. The concept of behavior modification was utilized to "shape behavior" in terms of the needs and demands of the group. This point of view accepts the ideas of reinforcement theory, behavior modification, testing, and remedial education.

2. **The needs of the individual.** Rousseau and Hobbes would represent philosophers who emphasized the "goodness of children" and the importance of the individual. This group believed in the idea of the "natural man" — the "noble savage." Rousseau did not believe that the child was waiting to be shaped by society or the environment —rather he felt that development occurred from within and happened as a result of interaction (on the part of the child) with the environment. He felt that children should be free to unfold, to explore the environment and to develop their abilities and capacities.

Early educators like Pestalozzi and Froebel, allied themselves with this point of view. Long before Montessori and Piaget, Rousseau emphasized "discovery." He once said, "Let the child know nothing because you have told him, but because he learned it for himself." Rousseau discussed four stages: infancy, childhood, late childhood and adolescence. He believed these stages would develop in an invarying sequence which was controlled by age and growth.

Contemporary researchers and teachers who tend to agree with this approach would study children through measurement and observation but in a natural, unstructured environment. Like Rousseau, and more recently Piaget, they would utilize a stage theory. (For an in-depth discussion of these early theories of child development the reader is referred to: Osborn, D.K. *Early Childhood Education in Historical Perspective.)*

While both points of view are important for an understanding of children, this book will examine some philosophical approaches which have had their historical roots in the writings of Rousseau and more recently in the works of Jean Piaget. We will focus our efforts on the individual and his needs as he grows and develops in terms of the intellect and cognitive functioning.

Purpose of the Book.

The purpose of this book is two-fold: One, to aid early childhood educators in understanding the intellectual growth of young children in preschool, kindergarten and the primary grades; and two, to equip the teacher with a group of tasks which will provide insight into the level and role of intellectual functioning.

An understanding of the nature of intelligence is of prime concern for persons involved in the education of young children. In order to understand the growth and development of learning and learning skills, teachers need to know how intelligence functions. Theories which are concerned with intellectual functioning are called cognitive theories. Cognition is the process by which one "comes to know." It involves the mental processes of imagination, memory, perception and reason. It is concerned with studying the way a person takes random stimuli from the environment and then organizes and processes this material into meaningful information. Cognitive-developmental theories raise the basic question: "How do children think?"

At birth the infant has no knowledge of the separateness of people and things in the environment. A preschool child has few logical reasoning skills as he enters an early childhood program. However, by the time he leaves the primary grades, he has made an important transition. The child has entered a stage of cognitive development which is characterized by logical reasoning skills and thinking more like an adult. In addition, the youngster possesses the ability to function with reasonable effectiveness in several academic areas.

However, there are many activities which are inappropriate for young children who have not yet made this transition. Teachers, administrators and curriculum planners seldom consider this factor in planning an early childhood curriculum primarily because logical thinking skills are very difficult to recognize and identify. One major factor which must be understood before investigating children's thinking is: Children do not think like adults. We cannot overemphasize this "truism." This is a concept which many adults do not fully understand or apply when planning programs for young children. Thus, if educators wish to assess the thinking skills of young children they must examine *How Young Children Think* before assessment will be effective and meaningful to the child and his teacher.

Historically, children were viewed as miniature adults. This belief led to the general idea that the only difference in the intellect of the young child and the adult was a matter of *quantity* of learning. Adults obviously possessed more information because they lived longer and experienced more and were therefore capable of complex thought.

However, research by Piaget and others provides evidence that this assumption is indeed, erroneous. We now know that the critical difference between the thought of the child and the reasoning of the adult is a matter of *quality* not *quantity*.

Children do not think like adults.

Roeper & Sigel (1967, p.78), provide an excellent example of the way a child might think in a given situation:

> John's family owns a puppy. John is about four years old. Blacky has been his constant companion and is being referred to as Blacky Jones, just as he himself is known as Johnny Jones. One day the family car, parked on a hill, rolls backward and kills the puppy, who is sitting behind it. John is heartbroken. His mother tries to make him feel better, explaining that it was an accident. Someone forgot to pull the brakes, and so, the car, rolling backward, ran over Blacky and killed him. Blacky should not have been sitting behind the car. When Mother

4

sees that John is still very unhappy, she
tells him that they may soon be able to
get another dog just like Blacky.

How well does John understand what his mother is
trying to tell him? How well is he equipped to understand
the meaning of this experience? Does John know what
death means? Does he know what life means? How can he
arrive at these concepts? Is everything that moves alive? If
so, the car that killed Blacky must be alive also and must
have decided to do it. Indeed the automobile might wish to
kill John, too, if he were to do something against the rules.
Does John understand that human beings can only produce
human beings? Or does he think if he (John) were run over,
would his parents soon get a new boy and forget him?

If the teacher is to be able to deal with the nature of the
child's thought processes, she must understand the level of
conceptualization which the child brings to the situation.
As we can see in the example presented above, there is much
room for interpretation and misinformation on the part of
the young child.

In the next section we will introduce the researcher, Jean
Piaget, who more than any other single individual, has
helped us understand how children think and the ways in
which their thinking differs from adults. His theories, and
their implication for teachers of young children, will be
examined.

Jean Piaget.

Jean Piaget (1896—1980), a famous Swiss psychologist,
brought a unique theoretical background to the field of
child psychology and development. As a youngster Piaget
was interested in birds, sea shells and fossils. By the age of
sixteen, he had published a number of zoological studies.
He studied biological sciences at the University of
Neuchatel (Switzerland) and earned his Ph.D. in 1918. His
dissertation dealt with the distribution of mollusks in the
Alps region. Soon afterward, he earned a second doctorate
in logic and philosophy. Following completion of this
degree, Piaget accepted a position at the Bleuler Clinic in
Zurich where he studied developmental psychology. During
this period he also studied psychoanalysis and the works of

Freud, Adler and Jung. Later Piaget went to the Sorbonne in Paris to further his studies on abnormal psychology. While in Paris, he accepted a position with the famous French psychologist, Theophile Simon, at the Binet laboratory.

Piaget became interested in children's thought processes, while working with Simon on the development of IQ test items. He was particularly fascinated by the children's incorrect, as well as their correct, explanations. Through his questioning Piaget became convinced that adults were not just "smarter" than children but that their thought processes were *qualitatively* different. Thus Piaget rejected Binet's *quantitative* definition of intelligence — a concept of I.Q. which is based on the number of correct answers given by an individual. Piaget began to devote his efforts to examining the modes of thinking of children. Feeling that their spontaneous responses provided clues to their innermost thoughts, Piaget developed a less structured interview procedure. For example, if a child became confused during questioning, Piaget would restate or rephrase the question. In order to trace the child's thought processes, he would probe further and analyze the response in greater depth. This method of study which Piaget called the *method clinique,* established the frame work for his theories.

In 1921, Piaget worked as a researcher in child psychology at the Rousseau Institute in Geneva. He also served as Director of the International Bureau of Education (Switzerland) from 1929 to 1967. In doing his initial pilot studies, Piaget observed the spontaneous behavior of his own children and obtained explanations from them. As he expanded his own research efforts, he began to study children of different ages to determine if they understood such phenomena as wind, rain and clouds; the floating and sinking of objects; and the concept of volume. Utilizing these observations he formulated and refined his theory of cognitive development.

With his co-workers he developed a variety of *tasks* which dealt with number, space, speed, time, physical quantity and classification. Piaget used careful recordings and observations as supporting evidence for his evolving theory on the nature and the development of intelligence. In 1955, Piaget founded the Center for Genetic Epistemology. *Genetic epistemology* studies learning processes by utilizing the disciplines of biology, philosophy, logic, mathematics and psychology. Piaget wrote over fifty books and hundreds of articles relating to his theories on intellectual development. He died in 1980 at the age of 84.

Most scholars, including Piaget himself, acknowledge that much of his theoretical material is difficult to understand. Piaget was, in essence, a research scientist who studied cognition, *per se.* Actually his theory is not an educational one — rather it is a theory of developmental psychology which deals with the nature of knowledge and the developing role of intelligence in humans. However, the theory has many implications for the educator and knowledge of the theory enhances the teacher's understanding of her children and the way that they think and grow and develop. As the teacher studies the material presented in this text, and as the teacher actually performs some of the "cognitive tasks" with young children, she will internalize the key features of Piagetian theory. We strongly believe that once the teacher understands the implications of Piaget's theory, she will never view children in the same way again. (Note: There are a number of books and articles by Piaget listed in the bibliography. Works which are starred (*) are particularly appropriate for educators.)

Key Features In Piaget's Theory

In considering Piaget's work, the teacher should be cognizant of several key points concerning his theory. These include:

1. **Children view their world differently than adults.** In an earlier section we made this key point when we related the story of John and Blacky. As we noted, "Children do not think like adults." Children have their own way of viewing themselves, of viewing others, and of determining reality. The manner in which they establish rules and organize their thinking is unique to childhood. Piaget' research demonstrates that the thought of the child and the reasoning of the adult is primarily a matter of *quality,* rather than *quantity.*

For example, Piaget says that young children are highly egocentric. (Note: Freud also uses the term, *egocentricism,* in a similiar, yet slightly different manner.) By egocentric, Piaget means that the child interprets events based on his own unique experience. He is not aware that others may have a point of view different from his own.

We remember Colin, a three year old in our nursery school, who was highly egocentric. He had great difficulty in learning to share. One day Colin hit Freida and took her doll. The teacher said, "Colin, that is Freida's doll!" Looking exasperated, Colin replied, "I know that, but *I want it!!*" A young child usually believes that others are experiencing identical thoughts and feelings to his own.

A young child often believes that she is the only person with a specific given name. For example, if a child has the name of "Sarah," she may believe that she is the only one with that name. One of our nieces felt this way. Even though she had an aunt named "Sarah," she felt this was her *own special name.* One Christmas she told the writer, "Guess what? Aunt Sarah has a stocking on her fireplace with *my* name on it!!"

Young children often view inanimate objects as alive. A two year old may believe that rocks, beds and tables are alive. A three year old will be convinced that "anything that moves" is alive. (In our story of John and Blacky: John believed that the automobile was alive. Further he was convinced that, in some fashion, the automobile had punished Blacky for disobeying a rule.) Brown (1979) found that most four year olds believed TV cartoon characters were alive and had feelings. The subjects in the Brown study reported: "When Bluto hits Popeye, it hurts him!" "If Mickey Mouse is cut, he *really* bleeds."

Children do not view rules and ethical matters in the same way as older individuals. Prior to four or five years of age, youngsters do not seem capable of moral reasoning. Between five to ten years of age, children view rules as sacrosanct and absolute. The child this age usually believes that rules come from God or some other authority figure like his parents or the teacher. Later, as youngsters grow older, they begin to develop a more realistic understanding of rules and of moral codes.

2. **The organizing process of cognition.** Piaget used several concepts to discuss the process of intellectual organization. These concepts — schema, adaptation, assimilation, accommodation and equilibrium are briefly reviewed in this section. For students unfamiliar with Piaget and his work, it is suggested that this section be read several times until the concepts are understood — since they are basic to Piagetian theory. For further study the reader is referred to Wadsworth (1971) and Cowan (1978).

Schema. Piaget believed there were two major structures in human beings: biological structures and cognitive structures. Schema is the term used to represent the cognitive structures. Schemas (some authors use *schemata* as the plural term), are the group of structures or concepts organized according to common features, which the child has or attains through experience and maturation. Perhaps the key to the concept of schema is the idea that the structures are *organized*. Information is stored in an organized fashion rather than in isolated form. It is the mental framework through which the child interprets his observations of the world about him.

Wadsworth (1971) has used the analogy of a card file. At birth the child has only a few cards on file. Through experience and maturation, new cards (structures) are added and old cards are refined and changed. For example, if the two year old has a large dog (and a corresponding category labelled "dog") and sees a cow — he would say "dog" since he has not developed a category (schema) for cows, horses, or other animals. After a number of experiences, the child will be capable of altering his cognitive structure and integrate a number of simpler structures (schemas) into a more complex one. Thus the child would ultimately develop several schemas concerning animals. Figure 1.1 illustrates this point.

FIGURE 1.1

Schemas Dealing with Animals

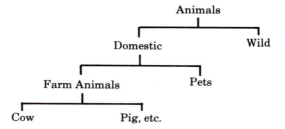

(Moos, eats grass, horns, long tail, gives milk, etc.)

NOTE: The complexity of the categories would depend upon the child's maturation and experience.

Adaptation, Assimilation, and Accommodation. As the child grows and adds new experiences, schemas change and become more complex. Piaget has borrowed the terms adaptation, assimilation and accommodation from the biological field and applied them to the cognitive structure of the individual.

Adaptation. This concept refers to the adjustment the person makes to environmental conditions. In the case of cognition, the individual must modify his cognitive structure (the schema) to make it more appropriately fit (adapt) the conditions of his environment. The individual can adapt in two ways: by assimilating new information into his current cognitive structure or by accommodating the structure (changing the schemas) in some way to make room for new information. Thus, when the child is confronted with new information he *must* make an adjustment (adapt). He adapts to the new situation by either assimilating it or accommodating to it.

10

Assimilation is the process of *taking in* new information and integrating this material into existing schemas. For example, if the child has some concept of "school" (a large building with trees and space around the building) and sees a neighborhood bank — he will try to fit this new idea into his existing schemas. In doing so, the child searches his previous experiences with buildings (examines his "card file"). Since this particular structure is unlike a house or a store — he makes the "best fit" possible and says, "There is a school!"

Accommodation is the second process which allows for schematic change. This is the process of *reaching out* and adjusting to new stimuli. In our example, let us suppose that the child sees a church but notices that it has a steeple, bells, long narrow stained glass windows, a cross, no playground and a sign in the front. Let us further suppose that the church building is sufficiently different so that he cannot accept it as a house, a store or a school. The child may query his mother, "What is that?" To her reply, "a church," the child may confirm, "a church" and thereby create a new schema to add to his existing cognitive structure. In accommodation, then, the earlier schema does not fit the new object and the child must create a new cognitive structure or modify an old one.

Once accommodation has taken place, the child again attempts to assimilate the object (the church). Since his cognitive structure has now changed (he has added a new "file card") he is able to assimilate the newly acquired concept of "church." The reader can see that when it is necessary for the child to make an accommodation to new stimuli, the process of assimilation is still necessary. Accommodation, then, is a process whereby the child "makes room" for a new concept to be assimilated.

Equilibrium. In many ways, equilibrium is the cognitive equivalent of the biological concept, *homeostasis*. The human body constantly strives to achieve a homeostatic balance. When the person is cold, he begins to shiver. This movement helps to warm the body. If the person gets too hot, he perspires. This action has a cooling effect on the body. When the body is tired, it demands rest. Thus, to achieve equilibrium, the body constantly adapts.

12

Whenever the child is confronted with an incongruous cognitive situation, he will attempt to adapt to it by assimilation or accommodation in order to restore a state of balance. The term, equilibrium, is used by Piaget to describe the process of regulating adaption (that is assimilation and accommodation). Equilibrium protects the individual from being overloaded with more information than he can assimilate or from attempting to accommodate to too many new stimuli. *Equilibrium is a self-regulating mechanism whereby the child can, himself, determine the rate at which he will acquire cognitive information.*

3. **Intelligence, or knowledge is constructed.** According to Piaget, the child constructs his own view of the world. This view is based on the child's personal experiences and how he perceives them. Piaget hypothesizes that knowledge is not passively received from the environment but actively constructed by the individual. Piaget held firmly that *all* knowledge, including logical reasoning, is constructed by the child as he responds to objects and interacts with people. Obviously the processes of adaptation (which includes assimilation and accommodation) and equilibrium help to determine the rate and the manner in which the construction takes place.

The child begins the process of construction in infancy as he creates his own perception of the world based on his experiences. Piaget observes how the neonate's reflexes adapt to external stimuli and become patterns through which the infant learns to recognize objects. He shows how the infant repeats these schemes but also slowly begins to differentiate his actions as the external situation changes. By acting on objects the infant begins to structure his own space and construct his own knowledge of the world around him. Through the experimentation of touching, tasting, holding, shaking, throwing, and dropping, the infant constructs knowledge which will later be useful to him.

From these experiences the child will construct generalized concepts which will aid learning. Initially some of these generalizations may be only partially true — but they will later be corrected as the child learns to differentiate through his experiences. For example: "All women are mothers" "All men teachers are daddies." "The soup is hot!" "After a few minutes (or if I blow on it), the soup will be cool." "I must stop the record *before* I remove it from the turntable." According to Piaget, it is from similar experiences and observations, that knowledge is constructed and logical thought emerges. Construction is a long process which begins at birth and continues throughout the life of the individual.

4.**Ways of acquiring knowledge.** We gain knowledge by discovery and investigation. Piaget noted *three* types of knowledge: physical, logico-mathematical and social.

Physical knowledge is acquired through physical activity. For example, the toddler picks up a block — he touches it with his mouth; he feels it with his fingers, he carries and stacks the block. Through this type of experimentation, the child gains knowledge of the object — its properties and its function. The source of physical knowledge rests mainly in the object. That is, in the way the object provides the child with opportunities for observation. (For example: A ball will roll; if a glass tumbler falls to the floor it will break.)

Logico-mathematical knowledge is gained through observation of the relationship between objects and interaction. The source of logico-mathematical knowledge relies mainly on the individual and the manner in which the individual *organizes* the reality. The child may observe a comparative relationship — Observing certain properties of a group of blocks the child may think — "This block is larger and heavier." However, he may also observe that all belong to the category of blocks — or that all are wood — or that they are all red. In this situation the conclusion is not based simply on observation but on the criteria which have been provided by the child himself. The relationship has been imposed upon and executed by the child. Kamii & DeVries (1978) provide an excellent description of physical knowledge and logico-mathematical knowledge in their book.

The third way in which knowledge is acquired is through social transmission. Individuals provide this knowledge to others through caring and social interchange. Social knowledge is obtained in a meaningful way as individuals interact in the "give and take" of everyday life situations. It is through social interchange that children acquire moral precepts and a knowledge of the feelings and attitudes of others. John Dewey, the famous educator, once observed: "We come to know an object when we know how it is made, and we know how it is made to the degree in which we ourselves make it." In the two sections which follow, we will examine how knowledge is actually acquired.

5. **Activity is a vital part of cognitive development.** Research suggests that most concepts cannot be meaningfully acquired without related activity. For example, reading about computers provides an individual with a basic, but relatively simple level of knowledge. However, in order to really internalize the operating features of a computer one needs "hands on" experience. *When one becomes mentally and motorically involved, learning and understanding are increased.*

Incidentally, this key point is also appropriate to the teacher in terms of her understanding of Piagetian theory. Merely reading this book will give you *some* knowledge. However, you must actively think, consider, evaluate and question in order to internalize these concepts. In addition, your knowledge will be vastly enhanced if you become *actively involved* with a child and utilize the *cognitive tasks* which are detailed in this book. We have had many students say, "Until I actually performed the tasks with the children, I did not *really* understand Piaget's theory!"

The same premise holds true for young children. They need plenty of mental and physical activity for learning to occur. An enriched learning experience involves *thinking* about a concept — questioning, challenging, hypothesizing, and evaluating. It also involves "hands on" physical activity — exploring, touching, holding and testing the material in order to fully understand its meaning.

All too often teachers merely *tell* children and expect them to internalize a concept. Our experience suggests that "telling" young children — as opposed to "involving" young children is generally a short-sighted approach. Activity — both physical and mental — is a vital part of cognitive development. Piaget (1973) noted: "It is absolutely necessary that learners have at their disposal concrete experiences (and not merely pictures), and that they form their own hypotheses and verify them through their own active manipulations."

6. **An enriched environment is a vital part of cognitive development.** This key feature is related to points four and five. Children need activity — but they also need stimulation and caring. They need adults who will provide enriched experiences which will challenge them to explore their environment. They need caring adults who will encourage them to test the hypotheses which make learning and problem solving possible.

Research shows that children need stimulation and nurturance for normal growth and development to occur. The early Iowa studies (Skeels, *et al,* 1983), showed the importance of an enriched preschool environment over the sterile atmosphere in an orphanage. The studies by Dennis (1960) showed that children who were largely ignored in an institutional setting were delayed in the mastery of motor skills. Bowlby (1951), and White (1967), reported similar results in children who remained in a hospital setting over a long period of time. Even in cases of mild deprivation, and in poor and unchallenging learning settings, children may fall nine to fifteen months behind youngsters reared under more favorable circumstances. In clinical cases where children have received little mental or motoric stimulation, where they have been abused and ignored; the effects have been disastrous. Often the deprivations have had long lasting effects — in some instances youngsters never recover from these debilitating circumstances.

In studies where children have been provided with a number of enriching experiences — opportunities to explore, to move around freely, to play, to be held and fondled by parents and other caregiving persons — development has either progressed normally or been speeded up. In a study by Clarke-Stewart and Apfel (1979), children with mothers who were highly nurturant developed earlier in cognitive areas. Notice that we are not talking about "pushing children" or over-stimulating them. We strongly believe that a "pressure cooker" environment can be as undesirable as a sterile one. The teacher and the parent can provide a balanced setting — but one which gives children challenging opportunities and ways of exploring the environment — ways which can stretch both mind and body.

7. **Play is important to the young child's development.** Play is fun and it is certainly an enjoyable activity for young children. However, play is also the "child's work" and it is his way of incorporating the world about him. Play is the vehicle for the assimilation and accommodation of new ideas and new concepts. Piaget felt that play was primarily assimilation — that is, the child makes the world "fit into" his own schemas — rather than having to accommodate to the demands of the world. Play serves as a reinforcer of ideas and patterns of behavior. Play enables the youngster to formulate ideas and then to test them. Much skill development occurs through play. The child often combines previously learned behaviors through assimilation and forms a new skill. Play with pots and pans, using spoons and other utensils, holding brushes and crayons, riding trikes, fitting puzzle pieces, carrying pillows and stacking blocks — all these activities help the child develop motor and perceptual skills; develop the ability to form spatial relations and the ability to learn skills with simple tools. These activities will be used, in a more sophisticated form in later life.

For the preschool and kindergarten child, play in the housekeeping corner provides an imaginative outlet. It gives the child a way to incorporate the everyday experiences of life. If the child has recently been to the hospital; if there is a new baby in the family; if there has been a separation, a divorce or a death in the family — all of these experiences can be "relived" and "evaluated" through creative play.

Older children can also use play to facilitate the process of adaptation. The teacher can provide opportunities for role playing, activity songs and other forms of dramatic play. Children can do creative problem solving through play. For example: "How did the Jamestown settlers feel during the cold winter of 1609?" "How can you solve the zoning problems of a shopping center?" "If several persons wish to use a certain item at the same time, how can we solve the problem of sharing in a fair and equitable manner?"

17

Stages of Cognitive Development

Piaget believed that cognitive development proceeded through a series of stages and phases. Within each stage certain developments took place in relation to the cognitive structures. While ages are presented for each stage and phase, these are only points of reference. As with all areas of growth, children mature at different rates. However, Piaget's research suggests that the sequential order of the stages and phases do not vary.

Piaget organized the levels or stages of cognitive development as follows: (1) Sensori-motor stage (Birth to two years). (2) Pre-operational thought (2-7 years). (3) Concrete operations (7-11 years) and (4) Formal operations (11 years to adult). Let us explore these levels of cognitive development in greater detail.

Level One: The sensori-motor stage. (Birth to 2 years).

The sensori-motor stage is the initial stage of cognitive development and occurs between birth and two years of age. Behavior is primarily motoric during this period. The child's experience seems to come exclusively through his senses. Early in this stage, response patterns are formed by chance combinations. Near the end of the first year of life the child may engage in anticipatory and intentional behavior. For example: The child will play "peek-a-boo" and begin to search for objects which have disappeared from view. While the child does not appear to think conceptually, one can see the beginnings of symbolic representation by the end of the sensori-motor stage. Some simple problem solving seems to occur through experimentation rather than via trial and error. As the child begins to develop language he begins to develop representational thought.

For the most part, information gained during this stage will occur *prior* to meaningful language development and will serve as the foundation for all subsequent understanding. Initially the infant will build on neonatal reflexes, and the development of thought will begin to emerge from these simple reflexive actions.

Piaget listed six phases in the sensori-motor stage. The table shows each phase and the approximate month in which the phases appear:

18

Table 1.1

PHASES IN THE SENSORI-MOTOR STAGE

Name of Phase	Age
1. Random Reflex actions.	birth-1 month
2. Primary circular reactions (first appearance of schemas).	1-4 months
3. Secondary circular reactions.	4-8 months
4. Coordination of secondary schemas and applications to new situations.	8-12 months
5. Tertiary circular reacitons.	12-18 months
6. Invention of new means via mental combinations. The appearance of memory & elementary planning.	18-24 months

1. **Random & reflex actions.** (birth — 1 month.) There is a continuation of the prenatal mode of living and the infant's behavior is completely autistic. (Note: In this text the term, "autism," is applied by using the usual dictionary definition — that is, "removed from any sense of reality; not possessing a reality orientation." Piaget uses the term in this manner and it is *not* being used in any clinical sense.) The child's experiences are primarily reflexive — sucking, grasping and looking; these serve to form the beginnings of learned behavior and personality development. During this period the child is able to distinguish patterns of light, dark, volume, and pitch.

2. **Primary circular reactions.** (1-4 months). During this period reflexive behavior will be replaced by volutional movement. The child attempts to make the world fit into his reflex patterns. Piaget believed that the first circular reactions to appear were a part of the infant's innate repertoire. In a "circular reaction" the initial response now serves as the stimulus for the second S - R sequence. During the second or third month, the infant *consciously* repeats behaviors which were previously reflexive. Thus, the infant performs an action and repeats it because it is pleasurable — and this action and reaction become repetitious. (For

19

example, shaking a rattle.) This repetition of behavior is a deliberate response and provides an *organized* (recognizable) pattern. (Notice the use of the term, "organized," represents the beginning of the growth of schemas.) The baby integrates experiences via sensory activity — sucking, smelling, holding — and new experiences become a part of this primary circular reaction.

The beginning of cause and effect occurs during this phase. Piaget (1957, 50) noted: "A child's first sense of causal relation is a diffuse connection between an action on the one hand and a result on the other without the comprehension of spatial relations or intermediary objects."

3. **Secondary circular reactions.** (4-8 months). The primary circular reactions continue but the schemas tend to be more repetitive and increasingly complex. The infant begins to imitate actions during this four month period. The child seems to be consciously aware of varying response patterns and simple cause and effect sequences begin to appear more frequently. Actions no longer simply occur, they are consciously created. Thus, in a secondary circular reaction the infant repeats an action because something occurred in response to the initial action. Piaget relates an incident in which he observed Lucienne, his younger daughter, shake her crib because she observed that this action caused the dolls in her bed to move. She became fascinated by this activity and repeated it for long periods.

4. **Secondary schemas.** (8-12 months). During this period the infant has changed dramatically in terms of physical growth. Most children will be able to sit up, creep and crawl. In the case of early maturers, they will be capable of walking alone. This increased mobility enables the child to effectively enlarge his horizons. He uses this period to consolidate earlier learnings and to expand his repertoire. Near the end of the first year of life the child begins to engage in anticipatory and intentional behavior.

Piaget relates the following example which occurred when his son, Laurent, was nine months old. Piaget hid a matchbox by placing the box behind a cushion and holding the cushion tightly. Laurent pushed his father's hand and continued to do so until Piaget finally moved it. The child then retrieved the matchbox. The youngster was able to show perseverance and finally reached his goal.

During this phase, children are capable of achieving *object permanency*. This concept may be simply defined as follows: The child has learned that an object exists even when it is not visible. (Prior to object permanence, it is a case of "out of sight, out of mind.") During this period the child begins to gain some understanding of "in front of," "in back of," "before" and "after." These rudimentary beginnings represent some vague awareness of spatial and temporal relations in their earliest forms.

By one year of age, most children can determine the *functional purpose* of an object. They will be able to distinguish that a rattle is something to shake; a ball is something you can roll; a dolly is something you hug.

While the child's conceptual ability is still quite primitive, he is capable of engaging in a number of complex behaviors. An adult may roll a ball toward the child. The child will get the ball, pick it up, walk over to the adult, return the ball and indicate his desire to have the adult throw the ball again.

5. **Tertiary circular reactions.** (12-18 months). (A more familiar term for *tertiary* is the "third order." Thus, this is the *third* stage of circular reactions.) In this phase the child repeats his actions but makes modifications which provide variety and diversification to the activity. Maier (1978) notes, "It seems as if children are saying to themselves, 'let's try it this time in a *new* way!'" As the toddler moves out into the world about him he enters a period of intense exploration. During this period the child makes many new discoveries — often to the parents' chagrin. The child may learn three *new* ways to throw food and five *new* ways to be negative. In his quest for new knowledge and variations on an old theme, the child is forced to devise new schemas and the process of accommodation takes place. In this period children become more aware of causality. Piaget relates the following incident with his son, Laurent, at thirteen months of age. While the boy was in his carriage, Piaget began moving the buggy with his

foot. Laurent leaned over the side of the carriage and, upon discovering the origin of the movement, looked at his father and smiled.

6. **Invention of new means.** (18-24 months). During this phase the young child begins to move away from the sensori-motor stage and one sees more evidence of cognitive development and behavior. In this phase memory and elementary planning take place. The toddler often thinks about an activity *prior to* pursuing it. He may even predict the consequences of a set of behaviors. We may hear the child as he "thinks out loud" and contemplates a course of action. For example: "Billie hit! Mama spank!!"

The two year old is aware of the existence of objects in their own right. For example, the child may see a coin roll on the floor and travel under the door to an adjacent room. By observing the child it quickly becomes evident that the youngster recognizes what has happened to the coin. He will open the door and begin to search for the coin in the next room. In this example we can see that the child has been able to solve a simple problem by projecting "what happened" and using his imagination to predict the outcome of the action he has witnessed.

The child's level of play is more complex. His language enhances play and his ability to remember situations enables him to model the behavior of others. We often see the two year old imitating the behavior of mother, father or an older sister or brother.

In this phase the child may engage in *deferred imitation;* that is, modeling a behavior which may have occurred in an earlier time frame. Several years ago the authors had a play group composed of children 18-24 months of age. One day Tommie was observed sliding down the slide backwards. He turned to the teacher and said, "Beverly slide this way!" The mother reported that indeed a cousin named Beverly had slid backwards — but this event had been observed by Tommie over three months earlier!

Level Two: Preoperational thought. (2-7 years).

The child makes many advances in the years between two and seven. There are tremendous changes in physical and social-emotional growth. In addition, there are dramatic changes in language development. However, there are still a number of limitations in the child's thinking ability which differentiate his thought processes from those of the teenager or the adult. Piaget uses the term, "pre-operational" to describe this stage because the child has not developed the necessary schemas for abstract thought.

The preoperational stage is often divided into two phases: the preconceptual phase (between two to four years) and the phase of intuitive thought (between the ages of four to seven). Sigel & Hooper (1968), have suggested that the phase of intuitive thought is actually a transitional period; between preoperational thought and the next stage, "concrete operations". At six or seven years of age, early maturing children may well give the appearance of concrete thinking in many situations.

Since most of this text is primarily concerned with cognitive tasks for children between the ages of two to eight years, let us examine this period in detail. We feel the teacher of young children should become expert in terms of how this age group performs in terms of physical, social-emotional, and cognitive development. By having a thorough knowledge of how the child grows and develops, how he thinks and feels, the teacher will be able to plan more effectively for the individual child and the group.

1. **The preconceptual phase.** (2-4 years). This is a period of rapid growth. The child between two and four years of age is an explorer. Everything is new to this youngster and his entire world seems full of exclamations. He exclaims, "Cat!" "Doggie!" "Truck!!" The child seems to enjoy making new discoveries and the world remains new and alive. The child seems to learn new words and expressions daily. However, even though the child and the adult use the same words — they do not necessarily mean the same thing. For example, the adult may say, "We share our toys." The child will mimic the adult and say to another, "We share our toys" — and then promptly grabs the toy from the other youngster.

A very important development occurs between the ages of two and four. The child is no longer restricted to his own perceptions and physical movement. He can employ a "mental picture" and use symbols to represent an object.

This ability is called the *symbolic function*. Utilizing this skill the child can create and retain a mental image to represent an object which is not immediately present. For example, the child may use a mental symbol of a doll or the word, "doll", to represent a doll. In addition to using mental symbols, the youngster begins to engage in symbolic play.

Physical. At two years of age the child has reached approximately fifty percent of his adult height. He has begun to walk, run and jump. However, his gait may be uncertain and the two year old may appear to "toddle" rather than walk smoothly. He can feed himself, drink from a cup, stack two or three blocks in series. By three to four years physical growth, particularly in terms of height, will have slowed down. However, motor development, both gross and fine, will proceed rapidly. If allowed to practice, some four year olds will be able to handle scissors, albeit not too accurately. Some will be able to copy a circle and a cross. Most children will be toilet trained, walk upstairs by alternating their feet, ride a tricycle and jump in place.

Social-Emotional. A great deal of activity takes place in terms of social-emotional development during this period. Erikson (1963) has characterized this period in terms of a sense of autonomy (2-3 years) and the early stages of a sense of initiative (4-5 years).

According to Piaget, one of the major characteristics of the preoperational child is his egocentricity. At two to three years the child is highly egocentric. The child sees the world only in terms of self. He is unable to imagine that life goes on when he is not around to see it. The youngster assumes that others see, hear and feel just as he does. He cannot conceive of being named any name other than the one he has. He is constantly searching to seek his own identity. *Me* is a word which often dominates his vocabulary and his actions. He often talks incessantly in a monologue even though nobody else is listening. For example, we may observe children in the sandbox engaged in parallel play who appear to be talking with each other. However, upon close examination, we will note that they are actually talking to themselves and seemingly unaware of the presence of any other child. Since the child seems to be exploring and discovering only in terms of self, he does not understand the concept of "sharing." As we examine the child's thought processes, we will see that he is incapable of the type of thought which would allow him to see a problem or situation from another person's point of view. The child knows the world only from his own particular frame of reference. He assumes that everyone else experiences the universe in precisely the same way that he does.

Note that the psychodynamic *theoreticians* like Erikson use the term, *egocentric*, in a similiar, but slightly different way than Piaget. The psychodynamic group uses the concept of egocentricity in a broader sense. They see the idea of "ego development" as central to the total development of the individual's personality. These ideas would be intertwined with the individual's concept of self, his self worth, his identity and self esteem. For most psychodynamic theoreticians, ego development during this formative period would have a profound effect upon all later personality development. For persons who would employ the psychoanalytic frame of reference, this period of time is *crucial* in terms of developing a healthy personality. The task for the parent, teacher and other caretakers is quite clear. It is important for the child to learn "Who am I?" and "What can I do?" It is also vital that the child develop good feelings about himself. It is necessary for the child to feel, "I am a *me* and it is alright to be the *me* that I am."

This early period (2-3 years) can often prove trying for the parent and teacher. The child cognitively begins to recognize the existence of others who are completely independent and "outside" of him. In addition, he may not wish their help or guidance in such mundane things as dressing, toileting or eating. He may protest loudly and firmly, *"I'll do it myself!"* Language is not sufficiently developed for sophisticated conversation. Coupled with the egocentric nature of the child and his vascillation between wanting to be both dependent and independent of the adult, the caretaker may indeed feel that this is the "age of the terrible twos!"

Play. The play of the child reflects this egocentric stage; this sense of autonomy, of discovery. The child hungrily uses all of his senses during this period. He touches, smells, tastes new objects. The light switch, pots and pans, blocks

— are all new and exciting. Play is the main occupation of the child of this age and it is the basic tool for adaptation. A major task for the parent and teacher during this period is to provide materials which the child can explore, manipulate, accommodate and assimilate into his own world.

Children's pretend play provides evidence of their ability to think symbolically. Youngsters may use a wooden block as a car, a train or a piece of fruit. During this period children assume a variety of roles in their symbolic play — they may become the teacher, mother or grocer. It is not unusual for children this age to assume the identity of another child — or even an animal. Three year olds can become a dog, a cow, a Smurf or Wonder Woman. When she was two years old, our daughter invented a playmate. Her name was Henry Kelly Cherry and *she* was "red all over!"

Language. Speech is highly egocentric in the preconceptual phase. As we saw in an earlier example, when children are engaged in parallel play they may be talking — but not directly to each other. In egocentric speech, the child talks in a monologue and appears to be "thinking aloud."

During this period the child acquires language and is capable of doing some representational thinking. Piaget uses the term, "preoperational" since he feels the child is incapable of using operational thought or logical reasoning. Language, through the use of verbal expressions and labels, begins to replace sensori-motor experiences. We will see the two year old using word approximations ("Coo . . ." for "Cookie") and telegraphic speech ("Cars go . . ." "Mommie eat . . ."). Note that the initial use of language is not symbolic; rather the words are usually related to ongoing actions, ("Billie hit!" "Allison bite . . .").

In addititon to word approximations, children may invent words to convey their ideas. Often certain expressions will have no meaning to an outsider. It is only as the child persists that the meaning becomes obvious. We remember a three year old who invented the word, "galoop" for doll and another child who referred to her grandfather as "pap paw." Children may make word combinations. For example: "Ho-motel" (a combination of hotel and motel); the "World's so Fair" for the "World's Fair" and "misdappear" for "disappear." As youngsters grow older their verbalizations become clearer and their words become more precise and restricted to more conventional speech.

By the end of the preoperational period, at six or seven years of age, the child will be capable of using complex language structures. Words will be used symbolically to replace the concrete object.

In the preconceptual phase four schemas seem to characterize much of the child's thinking:

(1) Children will be able to focus on only one attribute at a given time. Usually the child will *center* on the variable which stands out visually. He lacks the ability to coordinate variables. In a problem involving a change in a ball of clay, length stands out more than thickness, and the child will fail to coordinate the change of length with the change in width.

(2) The child is perceptually oriented. Events will be judged by their outward appearance. Piaget has demonstrated that perceptual judgment enters into the child's thinking about matter, space, time, number and causality. For example, the child at the preoperational level is likely to think that the number of objects in a set changes if the objects are bunched together rather than spread out. If you take a piece of cake and cut it into two pieces, the child will believe that he has more cake.

(3) The child has difficulty in realizing that an object can possess more than one property and thus can belong to several classes at the same time. A long red pencil can belong to the class of pencils, to the class of red objects, to the class of long objects, to the class of writing tools, etc., and one can live in Atlanta and in Georgia at the same time. This property of class is referred to as multiple classification.

(4) The idea of animism. Initially the child will believe that *everything* is alive. If he bumps into a table, he believes that the table kicked him. Later he will believe that "anything that moves is alive." An automobile is alive because it can move.

Before leaving this section, we would like to emphasize the importance of the preconceptual phase. Language experiences, personal-social development and play cannot be overemphasized. During this period the child is leaving the autistic world and moving into the world of socialization and reality. He needs a warm, loving and enriched environment if he is to maximize his opportunities for growth during this crucial period.

2. **The intuitive phase.** (4-7 years). In many ways this period, the phase of intuitive thought, is an extension and refinement of the preconceptual phase. There are some distinct differences, however. In the sensori-motor stage we saw the youngster passively accept the environment. He waited for others to come to him and minister to his needs. Now, during this period of development we see the child move out into his surroundings and react to the environment in a more realistic manner. We also see the growth and refinement of social participation and social interaction.

The child's ability to reason undergoes some changes during this period. In the preconceptual phase the child "reasons" in very concrete terms which are based on past experiences and simple memory. For example, the two year old may say, "Stove hot! Burn Ivan!!"

Children in the intuitive phase often make judgements and observations based on outward appearances. Piaget used the term, *identity constancy,* and believed that young children could not retain an original stimulus when superficial changes took place. Thus, if the physical appearance of a person or object changes, the child may be confused and disoriented. Using three to six year olds, DeVries (1969), conducted an experiment in which she placed a mask of a dog's face over the face of a cat. With the exception of some six year old children, most of the subjects in the study did not understand identity constancy and felt that the cat had either disappeared or "changed" into a dog. In a similar experiment, Kelly (1980), had a nursery school teacher "transform herself" to become Santa Claus. Most of the children accepted this transformation without question — even though they actually witnessed the transformation and assumed that the teacher was Santa.

As the child grows older he may use a type of reasoning which Piaget terms, *transductive.* Transductive may be defined as reasoning from one particular to another particular. In transductive reasoning the child sees a relationship between two concrete objects or events where one does not actually exist. For example, the child may reason, "I did not go to church, so it cannot be Sunday!" The child may incorrectly reason that one event is dependent upon a second event.

Intuitive children utilize *concatenative thought*. To concatenate means to unite, link or chain together. Piaget uses this term to describe the child's inability to analyze parts and place them in a larger, coherent whole. In concatenative thought, the child focuses on superficial qualities and attempts to chain them together even though none actually exist.

Piaget presents two types of concatenative reasoning: *syncretic* and *juxtaposition*. In syncretic thought the child attempts to make a logical explanation regardless of the circumstance. He attempts to reconcile, unite or combine opposing principles. For example: "Fish live in the water. They swim because God took away their legs. Goldfish swim faster than guppies because they are yellow."

In juxtaposition, one event is superimposed or placed next to another without apparent logical reason. For example: "I ate dinner because I am not hungry!" or "I must have washed my hands, because they are clean!" In juxtaposition the child recognizes that certain events are related (dinner, hungry; washing, clean) but fails to logically place cause and effect. Actually, in this instance, he presents the effect as the cause.

In the phase of intuitive thought, problem solving depends largely upon outward appearances and intuition. This phase ends when the youngster uses real concepts and begins to think in a logical and rational manner.

Physical. By the ages of four to six, most children will be excellent walkers, good runners and climbers. We would expect them to be able to jump forward and backward, hop on one foot and walk a four inch balance beam. Children this age (except for children with physical handicaps) should be able to zip and unzip a zipper, lace and tie their shoes and dress themselves. Their fine motor coordination will have progressed to the point that they can fold paper, cut with scissors, hold a paint brush or large pencil with thumb and finger. Most children will be able to copy small letters and simple geometric figures.

As children approach the end of this period (six to seven years), they will use this time to sharpen and tone up their physical skills. They may repeat tasks over and over again to attain mastery. They have the necessary skills to jump rope and play hopscotch. They usually enjoy climbing trees and playing rough and tumble games. Some children this age may have difficulty with printing and writing letters. Pencils are often gripped so tightly that the child may tire and frequently drop his pencil. Children this age have a longer attention span and can sit for longer periods of time. However, they are still easily distracted by outside disturbances.

Social-Emotional. One of the most significant events during this period is the expansion of social contacts. Many children will have moved beyond the nuclear family. Some will have attended Sunday school, nursery school or a day-care center. By five years of age, most of the youngsters will enter the kindergarten. In addition, children will have made trips to the grocery store, drug store and the shopping center. Many youngsters will have been on field trips to a farm or a fire station. As their social horizons widen, they will begin to lessen their egocentric behavior.

As the child enters the public school his concept of community enlarges and he may have friends and play-mates beyond his immediate neighborhood. He may spend the night away from home; he may join new groups (like the Brownies or Little League) which provide intensive relationships beyond the immediate family. The teacher often becomes the "superego ideal" and joins mother and father as a significant figure in the child's life.

Erikson (1963) characterized this period in terms of the sense of initiative and the beginnings of the sense of accomplishment. Psychodynamic theorists would state their position as follows: If the child has developed a good ego system and feels good about himself, he is able to "move out" and explore other vistas and other people. This feeling of ego strength, then enhances the move of making new social contacts. (In this instance the child might think: "I

30

am a *me* and I am happy with myself . . . therefore, I can now investigate and observe others and see who they are and what they can do.")

Language and play. In this section we are going to combine play and language since they are so closely connected in the phase of intuitive thought. Language can affect cognitive development in three ways: (1) The ability to engage in verbal exchange which leads to socialization with others. (2) The appearance of thought, i.e., the ability to internalize words and (3) the internalization of action. Thus, the child does not operate from a purely perceptual and motor base but can operate via pictures, symbols and mental experiments.

Piaget cites two types of preoperational speech: egocentric and socialized speech. As we saw earlier in our examples, egocentric speech often occurs in solitary or parallel play and is largely lacking in communication. It may occur when two children are talking but not directly to each other. In egocentric speech, the child is often uttering his thoughts out loud.

By four to five years of age, with the improvement of language, speech helps to make socialized play possible. We see children in the nursery school and kindergarten setting beginning to engage in associative and cooperative play. Motor and cognitive development go hand in hand and one sees block towers and complex structures emerge to become cities and neighborhoods. Children assume the role of train conductor, airplane pilot and bus driver. In the housekeeping corner scenes are enacted and the roles of mother, father and the sister in college emerge and become integrated into the child's world. In the sandbox mud pies are shared together and interactive conversations occur.

In the preconceptual phase we can hear one child say to another, "I know *you* want the trike, but *I* want it!" Later as the child's language improves and he understands the concept of turns and the value of playmates, we may hear him say, "You take the trike *two* times around the playground and then it is *my* turn!"

While five to seven year old children play together cooperatively, they are still highly egocentric and there are times when fights and arguments will occur. Verbal encounters can be quite violent because words are accepted as actual deeds and can take on a quality of absolute reality. Thus, a child may be extremely upset if another calls him "stupid" or "dummy." He may believe that being called "stupid" actually makes him stupid.

Teachers should remember the axiom, "The fewer rules you have, the fewer rules children will break." Piaget found that children this age have difficulty following rules. It is cognitively difficult for a kindergartner to concentrate on an activity, remember the rules and, at the same time, be aware of the teacher and the children. Our suggestion: Make a few rules and keep them simple!

The parent and teacher should also recognize that the child's verbal ability has outstripped his ability to comprehend. Children often use terms verbally, but have no real understanding of their meaning. They will speak and act as if they comprehend a particular event or concept. For example the child may say, "Two and two are four," and yet not understand the additive concept. He may say, "Next year I will be six years old," but the implications of this statement have little meaning. If parents and teachers are not cognizant of this trait they will expect performance from the child in areas where he is cognitively unable to deliver. *Remember that, regardless of the spoken word, thinking is primarily intuitive (as opposed to logical) at this age.* Piaget said (1955, 104): "Thought always lags behind action and cooperation has to be practiced for a long time before its consequences can be brought fully to light by reflective thought."

Level Three: Concrete Operations. (7-11 years).

Piaget refers to the third level of cognitive development as concrete operations. *Operations* can be defined as an internalized set of actions which permit the youngster to do mentally what he has previously done physically. Operations conform to the rules of logical thought and, as the child grows older, these cognitive operations become more advanced and sophisticated. In this stage operations are termed, "concrete" because the child performs operations mentally, but continues to think of *real objects* as he does.

In the sensori-motor stage, the child's world is based on simple perceptual cues and first hand experiences. During the preoperational stage, the child's perception is often based on magic and fantasy. In the concrete period the child begins to rely more on logic and rationality to utilize intellectual structures and to build cognitive experiences.

In the period of concrete operations the child can engage in thought that is reversible. This means that the child can mentally reverse the direction of his thinking. He recognizes that the parts and the whole are reciprocal. He knows, without physically performing an operation that something can be added to a group of objects and that something can be taken away from that same group. Near the end of this period, concrete operational children will be able to add, subtract, multiply and divide. However, they will need pencil and paper or other "helps" in order to make these computations. The ability to reverse thought processes gives the child increased conceptual ability. In relating an event he can go from the part to the whole and/or from the whole back to the part. The child can relate a story — be interrupted and then, following the interruption, return to the story and complete it.

Between two to five years of age children utilize direct experiences. In the concrete operational phase, however, the youngster is capable of concentrating on thinking about an event and its effects. In this stage thinking is mobile. The child can explain a fairly complex concept to another person. He is able to utilize ideas in his explanation rather than relying on actually showing the physical object.

Piaget points out that during the third stage of cognitive development, children are capable of conservation. For the reader who is unfamiliar with Piagetian terminology the word, "conservation," can be somewhat confusing. Conservation is the ability to recognize that an object remains the same despite a change in physical appearance. For example, a child with the ability to conserve liquid recognizes that eight ounces of water is the same whether it is in a small cup or a large pan. (Conservation is discussed in detail in Chapter 3.)

In the early part of this period (7-8 years), children can

conserve liquid, but not weight and volume. By nine years most youngsters will be able to perform simple problems dealing with liquid conservation "in their minds." However, in order to conserve weight and volume, ten year olds still need concrete materials for comparative purposes. Conservation enhances the child's conceptual ability. After developing the skills of conservation, youngsters are able to evaluate events by logic rather than by visual cues.

As the child develops and refines his ability to think logically, his horizons broaden tremendously. He has now moved from simple egocentric relationships and functional statements to being able to conceptualize a number of mental operations such as classification and seriation. For example, at two years of age the child will say, "Cookies . . . good!" "Cookies . . . mine!" But an eight year old will observe, "Cookies are round;" "Cookies can be chocolate chip or vanilla wafers — but they are *both* cookies." "Some cookies are large; some are small." "If I eat a cookie before dinner it will spoil my appetite."

In addition, the child is now capable of classifying objects by color, shape and size. He knows that there are hierarchies in classification. At this stage of development, the youngster is capable of arranging groupings in terms of quantitative attributes. This arrangement — in terms of length, width or weight is called *seriation*. Usually he will begin to seriate objects by color. Later objects will be sorted in terms of shape and size. Originally sorting occurs via trial and error and later through classification by kind and form. Piaget (1970, 31) notes: "Classification leads to seriation, first by constant comparisons, later by deduction." These findings have significant implications for the educator in the teaching of science, mathematics and logical reasoning. Children this age need *many* concrete opportunities which enable them to classify and seriate objects in terms of color, shape and size.

Erikson refers to this period of time (7-11 years) as the stage of industry or accomplishment. Children like doing tasks which give them a feeling of achievement. They enjoy pleasing their mother and their teacher. They are willing to do "small jobs" around the house like setting the table and running the vacuum. At school they enjoy the task of washing the blackboard and cleaning the erasers. The sense of industry is often reflected in skill improvement and in a feeling of accomplishment and acquisition. For example, youngsters this age enjoy collecting things like insects, bottle caps, candy wrappers and stamps. Children become preoccupied in classifying objects and search for systems of hierarchical relationships. Maier (1978, 57) notes: "These theoretical concerns find their application and become observable in children's play . . . for example, in collecting baseball cards, in making up stories of family intrigues, and in accounts of mystery stories which they view on television."

During this period of concrete operations we can observe intricate social structures and examples of ranked or graded classification systems in children's play. Children this age often establish club groups and social games with complicated rules and regulations. As an example the following set of rules were taken from a group of nine year old girls. These girls formed a club called, "The Secret Society of Young Females on Myrtle Street." The club rules follow:

1. Do not tell lies unless necessary.
2. Do not hurt anyone in any way.
3. Do not tell a black lie, ever.
4. Do not curse at all.
5. Do not make faces, except at Ronny.
6. Do not be selfish.
7. Do not tattle, except on Ronny.
8. Do not make a pig or hog of yourself.
9. Do not be grumpy, except to Ronny.

Level Four: Formal Operations. (11 years to adult).

The fourth level of cognitive development, formal operations, occurs near the onset of adolescence after the child has left the primary grades. (Note: Some persons have assumed Piaget meant that by eleven years of age, the child graduates into "adult thinking." While the young person begins to use an adult mode of thought, and the process of thinking is more mature, teenage youngsters still lack the experience and *savior faire* to approach "full blown" adult conceptualization.)

Twelve year olds will be able to do addition, subtraction, multiplication and division. However, while they can make computations with whole numbers, many twelves will have difficulty with decimals and fractions. Many twelve and thirteen year olds will still be unable to do "word problems" and "mental arithmetic." As the adolescent grows older (15-17), he will be able to read passages of prose and poetry and determine the author's intent.

At this stage the youngster is capable of dealing effectively with advanced abstract levels of thought. This higher order of thinking involves deductive reasoning, thinking about thinking, and working with theoretical constructs. For example, the teenager can engage in higher order conceptualization. He can imagine the fourth and fifth dimension, a hypothetical construct or an intervening variable — as opposed to concrete thought where an item must be "in sight."

In the third cognitive level, children can deal with the world in *real* terms. Concrete operational children can discuss a situation "as it is." However, in the formal period of development, the adolescent can approach problems from an idealistic, as well as a realistic point of view. Most high school students can talk "in an adult manner" concerning a situation "as it is" and "as it could be." Adolescents seem to enjoy deep philosophical discussions on sex, future vocations, human relations and world politics.

Thinking, in the level of formal operations, is more flexible and systematic. It is possible for the youngster to examine a problem from several vantage points and imagine a variety of possible solutions. However, there are still "gaps" in the child's thinking. For example, his lack of in-depth experiences and sophistication may prevent the teenager from understanding the nuances of life's complexities. In addition, his own social immaturity makes it difficult to place events which effect him personally into the larger perspective. His adolescent egocentricity usually allows him to place his own selfish interests above those of the family. His reliance on the peer group may cloud his ability to think rationally — he may go against "rational thought" and comply with the demands and wishes of the peer group.

Charles (1974, 23), presents a typical picture of the reasoning level of the adolescent: "Our student has become a full-blown theoretician. If not accurate, he is at least prolific. He composes theories about everything. Everything has an explanation, a place. Prescriptive theories of right and wrong abound." In this stage the person has the potential to become a mature individual who, over time, will be capable of developing a personal value system and a mature sense of moral judgement.

Rules and Moral Development

Piaget was also fascinated with the manner in which children develop a sense of right and wrong and establish ideas about lying and stealing. In his book, *The moral judgement of the child,* Piaget discusses rule making and the development of moral values. Piaget developed his theories about moral behavior by watching children play games. As a part of his research he carefully observed several groups of young boys playing marbles and acquired a thorough knowledge of the rules of the game. Piaget believed rule making and moral development were intrinsically related. He felt that the essential feature of morality was the acceptance of a system of rules.

Like cognitive development, Piaget believes that morality progresses through successive stages. These stages are: (1) The premoral stage (birth to 4 years), (2) Egocentric stage (4-7 years), (3) Incipient cooperation stage (7-10 years), (4) Genuine cooperation stage (11 years to adult). Kohlberg (1963) has suggested several revisions and extensive modifications to the Piagetian stages of moral development. We believe that an examination of both theories can be helpful to the teacher. This material is discussed in detail in Chapter Eight.

Levels of Development: A word of caution.

As we indicated earlier in this chapter the ages used to indicate the levels of thought are approximate and are, in essence, only points of reference. While Piaget viewed cognitive structures developing in a continuous, invariant sequence (and research tends to support the view that acquisition of concepts is hierarchical), there are individual differences. The rate of development will vary between children. As with any area of development, there are early and late maturers. In addition to maturation, individual experience effects development. Thus, every child will not learn to conserve on exactly the same date at exactly the same time.

Each stage of development depends upon the earlier stages. Erikson (1963) and Havighurst (1972) have pointed out that each stage is laid on the foundation of the preceding one. Maier (1978, 29) also notes some additional attributes of cognitive development:

> Each stage entails a period of formation and a period of attainment. New patterns of thinking, constituting a new provisional equilibration, replace previous levels of cognition. These changes are cumulative and irreversible.

> The sequence of development . . .creates a hierarchy of cognitive experience. Each novel pattern entails a more complex and effective form of cognition. Once a new form of thinking is achieved, the capacity to do so leads to new and advanced perspectives of cognition. Each developmental period is defined by new questions, and, concomitantly, each cognitive acquisition poses new questions.

Sigel (1964) pointed out that although cognitive growth appears to be a continuous process, it proceeds in discontinuous ways with spurts and plateaus of achievement. There is also a significant overlap between stages and the individual child is constantly in a state of transition (on certain items) as he progresses toward the next stage of development. At times the teacher will observe a child in the process of transition. During this period the child may provide an incorrect answer initially, but upon questioning may give the correct response or even "flip-flop" answers if requestioned.

As mentioned earlier in the chapter one of the major purposes of this text is to provide the teacher with a group of cognitive tasks adapted from Piaget's studies. The following chapters will explain the tasks in detail and suggest ways to present them to young children. Through the administration of these tasks the teacher will gain insight into the cognitive ability of the child. This appraisal of the child's cognitive functioning will aid the teacher in structuring the curriculum and planning learning experiences appropriate to the child's ability and intellectual level.

CHAPTER TWO

Techniques for Administration of Piagetian Tasks

In Chapter One we pointed out that Piaget designed a number of experiments which provide insight into the child's mode of thinking. In essence, these experiments are actually a series of exercises (often referred to as "cognitive tasks") which children perform that can effectively assess their thinking skills. Fortunately, these tasks are relatively easy to administer and can be given by a teacher if she will follow a few simple procedures.

This text has *two* sets of tasks. Set I is primarily designed for children from two to nine years old, but can be used with children up to twelve years of age. These tasks, *numbered* 1-29, focus on conservation, classification, temporal relations and spatial relations. Set II is designed primarily for children in the concrete operational stage and in the early stages of formal operations — ages 7 to 14 years. These tasks focus primarily on logic, reasoning, and moral development. The tasks in Set II are *lettered* from A-K. The teacher may wish to administer only selected tasks from Set I or Set II — depending upon the particular child.

In some cases it may not be possible for the teacher to actually administer the tasks to the child. Our experience has shown that a parent or an aide can be trained to examine the children. If it becomes necessary for someone other than the child's teacher to administer the tasks, a thorough demonstration, with explanation, is necessary for accurate information to be obtained. When, where and how to administer the items are crucial questions for the examiner to consider. [Note: When reading this chapter you may wish to refer to the Cognitive Task Protocol Form in Appendix A and to the sample protocol ("Ocie T") in Appendix C]. The suggestions made in this chapter will help insure that the assessment of the child will be reliable and accurate.

General Suggestions.

If the Piagetian tasks are to be meaningful to the teacher she needs the child's best efforts. Prior to presenting the tasks to the child the examiner should have established good rapport. The examiner shoud be prepared to spend sufficient time with the child so that the youngster will feel safe and secure. Thus, it is not advisable to test the child the first days of class. Instead, the examiner should wait until the class has "settled down," the teacher is in control, and the children are comfortable. If a child is busily engaged in an activity, the examiner should not remove the child from the enjoyed activity but rather wait until the child is finished or suggest doing the tasks when the child is otherwise unoccupied.

It is not necessary to administer all the tasks to the child in a single period. If the child tires of the tasks, the examiner should discontinue for that day. When the child is tired or bored he will often give the examiner any type answer just to bring the questioning to a quick conclusion.

Where possible, the testing should be conducted in a room away from the other children. Ideally the examining room should be free of distracting materials. It should be simply furnished, well lighted and contain a small testing table plus one chair each for the child and the examiner. If a testing room is unavailable, the examiner can set up a table in the corner of the classroom. In some cases, however, there may be children who are too easily distracted by normal room activity and the tasks may have to be administered when the rest of the class is outside or away from the room.

The examiner will need a clip board, two or three pencils and the necesary protocol forms for recording the results. A clip board provides a hard surface for recording answers, verbalizations, observations, and behavior on the protocol.

A clip board also enables the examiner to write at an angle, making this activity less distracting. [Note: The protocol in Appendix A may be reproduced by classroom teachers for use with students, without obtaining prior permission. Large protocol forms (8½" x 11") are available and may be ordered directly from the publisher.]

Most of the materials needed for administration of the tasks are common, ordinary objects which can be easily obtained and assembled for each individual test. In some cases, the teacher may wish to make a substitution if another item is more readily available. (For example, in Task #7, buttons are suggested. However, the teacher could also use colored pieces of construction paper, small blocks or colored discs.)

Materials for each task should be assembled ahead of time. We would suggest that small boxes be procured for each task and the necessary materials placed in boxes and labeled. Even though the materials are everyday items, we should forewarn the teacher that it may require some time to assemble the entire kit. If others are using the cognitive tasks to assess their pupils, we suggest putting together a *master kit* which could be made available for use by the entire group.

Whenever the child completes a task, the examiner should immediately remove all of the test materials from the table. If this is not done, most children will continue to play with the items, thereby unnecessarily lengthening the testing period. (Note: This suggestion is not an absolute rule. In some instances, the examiner may feel that the child would be upset if the materials were "summarily removed." In such a situation, it may be advisable to let the child play with the materials for a few minutes.) Usually, if the tester states that she is going to remove the materials —and makes this statement in a definite manner with a firm voice, the child will readily comply to the request. For example:

a) "I am going to put this material away now."
   rather than
b) "Don't you think it would be better if we put this material away now and I will try to find something else for you."

The examiner should study each task thoroughly and be familiar with the purpose of the task., questions to be asked, and the requestioning procedure. Often inexperienced testers waste time and thereby reduce the child's level of motivation. If the examiner does not know the materials, the tasks can quickly become unclear and indefinite. For example:

    a) "The next thing I would like to do is . . . "
       rather than
    b) "Just a minute, I think maybe we should try this . . . no, let's see . . . perhaps we should . . ."

We cannot overemphasize this point; it is extremely important for the tester to be thoroughly familiar with the materials and the procedures. By having a detailed knowledge of the cognitive tasks, the examiner will be able to place the child at ease and proceed in a more expeditious manner.

The examiner will note that the tasks have been constructed so that only one question is presented at a time. This is important since a "double question" can be misleading to the child. The examiner may wish to vary the questions to fit a particular group of children. Note: In a standardized testing situation, the examiner *always* asks questions in the same way. When presenting cognitive tasks, the questioning procedure is different. The tester should remain flexible in framing questions. Items may be reworded and rephrased as necessary. In addition, the examiner should probe in some detail in order to gain a deeper understanding of the child's responses and ascertain the child's intent. This procedure assumes an attitude of questioning and inquiry rather than presenting a set of standardized questions. However, care must be taken that the wording of a question does not suggest an answer to the child. For example:

    a) "Which rod (stick) is longer?"
       rather than
    b) "I think both sticks are still the same, don't you?"

The key to making an accurate assessment of the child's cognitive skills lies in the questioning technique. If an examiner is unclear as to the child's answer or his reasoning—

ask the question again; rephrase the question, or say, "tell me more," "Why do you say that?" or "Yes, and what else?" In many cases the child's additional explanation will be more meaningful than the initial answer and may provide the examiner with insight into the child's thinking processes.

Pay particular attention to the child's *style* of response. Let us suppose that the examiner may ask: "Which stick is longer?" To this question, the child might respond, "That one." However, in the examples presented below we can readily see that a specific response may have several possible interpretations.

   a) The child may respond in a querying manner: "That one?"
   b) He may respond in a hesitant manner: "T-The-The-That one?"
   c) He may give the tester a broad, knowing smile and a firm, resounding reply, "That one!!"

In this example, the sensitive examiner will note that the style (manner) of the response makes *all* the difference. In (a), the child may actually not know the answer and queries the examiner for help. In (b), the child is probably in transition. In both (a) and (b), more probing is indicated in order to more fully understand the nature and intent of the response. In (c), it appears that the child knows the concept in question.

The examiner is also reminded that there are no "right" or "wrong" responses to the tasks. Upon receiving a response to a question the examiner should positively reinforce the child. This action can be accomplished by smiling, nodding or saying something like, "yes," "That's fine," "Alright." The examiner should avoid frowning, shaking her head or looking disgusted since these actions may unknowingly cause the child to feel failure and inadequacy. (Note: In Set II there are some math problems which do have a specific answer and older children may recognize that they have not answered a question correctly. If this situation occurs, the examiner should assure the child that she is only interested in the subject's approach to problem solving and that there is no "score" or "passing grade.")

44

As with all areas of teaching, clarity is important in presenting the tasks to the child. The examiner should be certain that the child understands what is expected — it is important that the questions be made clear to the child. In addition, the examiner should not present the child with a choice unless she clearly intends to give the child a voice in the matter.

The Tasks

As mentioned earlier, there are two sets of Tasks contained in this text. Set I is primarily designed for children two to nine years old. Set II is designed for children in the concrete operational stage and in the early stages of formal operations — ages seven to fourteen years.

Set I of the Tasks.

Four chapters in the book are devoted to a discussion of four major areas studied by Piaget. These are: conservation, classification, temporal relations and spatial relations. The first part of each chapter is devoted to a discussion of the specific area. The last part of the chapter presents tasks designed to help the teacher determine the extent of the child's cognitive development in the area under consideration.

The tasks in Set I are *numbered* and a total of twenty-nine tasks are presented: Tasks 1-12, conservation; tasks 13-20, classification; 21-24, temporal relations; and tasks 25-29, spatial relations.

In the protocol there are three major categories for recording the results of each specific task. These are UC, NH, and T. After the subject performs a specific task the examiner should circle UC, if the child *understands the concept;* NH, if the child cannot perform the task (needs help); and T if the child is in the *transition* stage. The examiner will note that some tasks (13-16; and 28) do not contain the T category. Each task lists simple critieria to help the examiner make the appropriate judgement.

Set II of the Tasks.

Chapters Seven and Eight discuss reasoning and moral development. The first part of the chapter is devoted to a discussion of the specific area. The last part of the chapter presents tasks which help the teacher have a fuller understanding of the child's logical skills and level of moral reasoning.

The tasks in Set II are *lettered*, A-K. Tasks A-G are presented in Chapter Seven. Tasks H-K are contained in Chapter Eight. Tasks A to E contain problems which yield a specific answer. There is no "T" category, "in transition," for the Tasks A to G. The teacher should record these tasks as follows: A correct response is scored as UC — understands the concept. An incorrect response is scored NH —needs help. The teacher should probe to determine how the child arrived at his answers. The child's verbal response usually provides important clues to his knowledge (or lack of it) concerning the problem in question.

Task F (the proverbs) and Task G (the syllogism) are recorded UC or NH. UC would indicate that the child understood the proverbs and the syllogism. NH would indicate that the youngster either answered incorrectly or did not understand the proverbs and/or the syllogism.

Tasks H, I, J, and K (Chapter 8) deal with moral reasoning. Symbols UC, T, and NH, are not used for these tasks. The examiner should record the child's responses in her *observation notes* and compare these statements with the stages of Piaget and Kohlberg which are presented in detail in Chapter Eight. Note: In this text we refer to the written notes which are made by the examiner as "observation notes."

Cognitive Style.

The manner by which persons perceive, interpret, and respond to a given situation can vary greatly. Kagan (1964) and Sigel (1972) have referred to this approach as one's *cognitive style*. The research in this area suggests that some children tend to be impulsive; others reflective in their approach to problem solving.

Messer (1976) found that by five to six years of age, a child's cognitive style is fairly stable and changes relatively little over time. Impulsive children tend to blurt out the first thing which comes to mind; they act impulsively and give little thought to a problem. The impulsive child often takes the easiest approach to a situation and fails to consider other possible alternatives. Reflective children, on the other hand, are more precise in their approach to problems — they are more analytic and tend to consider a variety of possibilities before settling on a definite course of action.

There are some tests available which will measure the child's cognitive style. They are relatively easy for the teacher to administer. Kagan (1965), devised a Matching Familiar Figures Test which provides clues to the reflectivity and impulsivity of children. The Learning Style Identification Scale (LSIS) by Malcolm, *et al* (1982), identifies five styles of learning. Our own experience has shown that most sensitive teachers can usually recognize impulsive and reflective youngsters after the first few days of class. Suggestions to help teachers recognize the child's style of learning and to utilize that knowledge are mentioned in Chapter Ten and in the works of Kagan and Malcolm.

A task which will determine cognitive style is presented at the end of this chapter. It is adapted from Kagan's Matching Familiar Figures Test and provides the teacher with some insight into the child's learning style. If the teacher wishes to administer this item, it may be recorded on the protocol under question three, in the *General Observations* section. This item is listed as: *Cognitive Style:* R — I. If the child's approach was reflective the examiner should circle the "R." If the approach was impulsive, the examiner should circle the "I."

General Information on Recording.

Insofar as possible, the examiner should record the child's responses *verbatim*. (Note: In the text we refer to these written responses as "observation notes.") This technique enables the teacher to study language patterns and vocabulary. Since young children often "think out loud," *verbatim* material gives the teacher insight into the child's thought processes. The child who continually says, "I don't know," may actually be using this statement as an avoidance technique. The child who continuously talks during the testing situation or constantly changes his answers may also be exhibiting avoidance. Through the use of "observation notes" the teacher can observe patterns of thought which might not be evident otherwise.

The protocol does *not* provide space for the observation notes. Therefore, the examiner will need extra paper for recording the child's answers. In addition, most testers find that a tape recorder is invaluable for writing the final report. (Refer to the Ocie T. protocol in Appendix C. This sample protocol shows how observation notes enhance and enrich the total testing report.)

In addition to recording the results of the tasks, the protocol includes a section entitled, *General Observations*. This section contains the following questions:

1) How did the subject relate to the examiner?
2) Did subject perseverate? (That is, experience difficulty in moving to new tasks.)
3) Cognitive Style: Circle R I. What was the subject's general approach to problem solving?
4) How did the subject react to apparent success? apparent failure?
5) If frustrated, how did the subject react?
6) Special observations in terms of vocabulary.
7) Did the subject evidence visual problems?
8) Did subject appear to hear clearly? Use normal voice? Did the instructions need repeating? If so, how often?
9) How did subject's general approach to the tasks compare with the rest of the group?

To the question, "Can I compute a final test score?" The answer is "No." Unlike IQ tests, there is no final score. Most IQ tests are based on a quantitative definition of intelligence—that is, a child's IQ is reflected in the number of correct responses he makes. The writers of the text feel that a "test score" of this type is of little value to the teacher. The purpose of the tasks is to help the teacher understand the modes of thinking and the child's general level of cognitive development.

Since children are presented the tasks under relatively similar circumstances some general comparisons are possible. With added practice the tester will attain more proficiency in the techniques of questioning. We feel that as the teacher examines the protocols she will derive information which will help her plan the curriculum for the individual and the total group. The text does discuss types of activities which will be helpful in enriching children's experiences.

Another question many people ask after administering the Piagetian tasks is, "Why not simply make the child memorize the concepts?" While it is true that the teacher can *finally* get a child to "parrot back" a specific response, this type of learning is usually transitory. Piaget believed that knowledge had little meaning when it was passively provided by the adult. His observations showed that children construct conceptual information via active involvement. Children alter their perceptions *gradually* through the process of construction and this process usually takes place over an extended period of time.

The child does not change his beliefs overnight, or as a result of information gained through "mass memorization." Since material learned by rote was not internalized via construction, the child will return to his own "logical" reasoning and cite the same answer he gave previously. The end result is wasted time (for teacher and child) since verbal learning of this type merely teaches the child to give the correct response by rote memory without actually understanding the logical implications of his response.

The information obtained from the administration of these tasks may be used to help formulate a curriculum for each child which is appropriate for his cognitive level and style of learning. To push a child beyond his cognitive ability has been labeled the "American question" by Piaget. He states that it has only been in the United States that he has been asked, "How can I teach these skills sooner or faster?"

It is the authors' view that the correct environment, the teachable moment and leading the child to broaden his experiences on a concrete level will best achieve cognitive goals for each child in his own good time. The tasks presented should prepare the teacher to analyze a child's level, determine appropriate expectations and design curriculum goals which will build on the child's cognitive growth and development.

Suggested Assignment.

In Chapter Two, a discussion is presented on the administration of a group of cognitive tasks. These tasks are particularly appropriate for children over two years of age. In order to help the reader understand early cognitive development (from birth to two years), the following assignment is presented:

1. Make a process recording of at least two infants between birth and one year of age. (A process recording is one in which the observer records the child's actions and activities.) At the beginning of your observation describe the child's general appearance and demeanor in detail. Is the infant active, passive? Does he smile, use sounds or word approximations? Is the infant rolling over, sitting up, crawling? If possible, determine the actions or reactions as described in Piaget's sensori-motor phases. (Refer to Table 1.1)

   a. Is the infant's behavior reflexive?
   b. Does the infant appear to consciously repeat behaviors and can one discern organized patterns?
   c. Does infant imitate actions of others?
   d. Is the infant capable of object permanence, perseverance?

2. Observe at least one child between one and two years of age. In addition to the general description of the child described in (1), here are some specific suggestions:

   a. Do you see any evidence of new schemas, new assimilation and accommodation to behaviors?
   b. See if the youngster can predict the consequences of a simple action. (You may have to ask the parent if the child is capable of predicting simple behaviors. For example, does the child make statements like, "Stove hot. Burn Michelle." or "Rover bite Ronnie! Make Ronnie cry!" "Daddy come home after snack time?")
   c. Do a simple activity with the child. (Rolling a ball, stacking blocks.) How does the child react? Can he follow simple directions? Can he interpret *two* directions? (Example: "Take the ball to your mother and then bring me the newspaper.")

TASK TO DETERMINE COGNITIVE STYLE

Task: Cognitive Style

Materials:

Use illustration in Appendix B.

Situation:

Say, HERE IS A PICTURE OF SOME LADYBUGS. SEE THE LADYBUG AT THE TOP? (Point to the ladybug at the top of the illustration.) SHOW ME ANOTHER LADYBUG IN THE PICTURE WHICH IS *JUST LIKE* THIS LADYBUG.

Requestioning:

The examiner should *not* provide any hints. The method of response is crucial to the scoring of this item. If the child responds quickly — smile and say something like, YES, YOU PICKED THAT LADYBUG — and then move on to the next task. If the child says something like, "This is hard," or "They all look alike," the examiner may say, YES, IT IS HARD . . . BUT SHOW ME ANOTHER LADYBUG JUST LIKE THIS ONE.

Appraisal:

- I Impulsive. Child sees all ladybugs as alike. Quickly chooses a ladybug, shows little interest in closely analyzing the other ladybugs. Appears to make a snap judgement.

- R Reflective. Takes time. Attempts to eliminate other ladybugs via some type of logic. Uses close scrutiny. Compares pictures slowly.

Comment:

Note: The child does *not* have to make the correct choice to score (I) or (R). The judgement is made on the style or approach the child takes to solve the problem. (Refer to earlier section in this chapter.)

The reflective child carefully studies the various parts of the object, he takes his time and responds more slowly than the impulsive child. The impulsive child often makes a quick judgement and gives the first answer which "comes to mind." *Scoring:* This item is scored in the General Observations section under question three. If the child's approach was impulsive, circle the "I". If the child's approach was reflective, circle the "R."

CHAPTER THREE

Conservation

Most of Piaget's original writings are in French. As a result, there are times when translators substitute words which may have different meanings for the American reader. The word, *conservation,* is such a term. Americans usually think of *conservation* in the ecological sense — that is, "Conservation is the careful preservation and wise management of our natural resources." In Piagetian terms, however, *conservation,* is the ability to recognize that an object remains the same despite a change in physical appearance. Thus an object will maintain certain characteristics in the face of other superficial changes. (It is unfortunate that the translators of Piaget's works did not use the term, *retention.*) Piaget views conservation as a key prerequisite for the development of logical thought. He also feels that conservation is the foundation upon which children learn the logic of mathematics and other rational relationships. In his research Piaget examined objects and substances in terms of length, width, number, mass, area, weight and volume.

Before attaining the ability to *conserve,* The child's thoughts are guided by his own perceptions. It should be noted that a child's perceptions are ruled by his own thinking processes and are not like those of an adult. He draws conclusions, but is usually unaware when his conclusions contradict one another. Let us examine the development of conservation in young children. A newborn enters the world with no concept of himself as being distinct from his surrounding environment. The infant considers his mother to be an extension of himself. During the sensori-motor period, the child begins to slowly separate his own being from his environment and builds the idea of objects around him. He eventually discovers that objects continue to exist even when they are out of his sight ("permanence of object"). The child also begins to believe that objects remain the same in shape and size ("object constancy"). The knowledge that a favorite toy remains the same size and shape in other settings and, even when out of sight, the toy still exists, is a profound discovery to the infant.

There is a very rapid increase in the rate of learning after the onset of language which includes many concepts dealing with amount and quantity. Maturation and experience, coupled with an increasing vocabulary, lead the child to ask for "a tiny bit of broccoli" and "a big, big piece of cake." He begins to understand that when he adds sand to his bucket . . . "he has more" and when he takes sand out . . . "he has less." One might erroneously think that the child who understands this concept understands conservation. However, few children enter school with a complete understanding of conservation and most do not develop such understanding until the age of six or seven; some not until eight years of age.

The key to conservation appears to be centration. The preoperational youngster fails to conserve because he "centers" on only a part of the total amount of information which is available to him. Thus, the child concentrates on a single attribute — for example: length, width, mass, or area and fails to incorporate the whole.

There are three stages in conservation. In stage one children do not conserve; they see one dimension as dominant. Stage two is the period of transition. In the second stage, children begin to understand the quantity being conserved — but vascillate upon requestioning. In the third stage the child can follow the transformations and conserve.

An analysis of one of the Piagetian tasks will help to clarify the stages of conservation. In Task 3 (see this task at the end of the chapter), the examiner gives the child two similar balls of clay. Most four and five year olds will agree that both balls are "exactly the same." However, when the examiner rolls one ball into the shape of a hot dog — the child will now state that the "hot dog has more clay." In stage one the child *centers* on the attribute of length and is unable to recognize that no change in quantity has taken place. In the second stage, when children are in a period of transition, their replies will reflect their uncertainty. Initially, they may state that the quantities are the same. However, upon requestioning, they will change their mind and state that the hot dog is larger. In the third stage, children are able to follow the entire procedure and remember (conserve) the earlier shape of the clay balls. When the child is able to understand that the change in shape does not effect the quantity of the material, he is able to conserve substance.

Piaget found that the concepts he studied varied in difficulty. Piaget used the term, *horizonal decalage,* to describe this phenomenon — that is, the child learns to conserve various attributes at different rates and times. (Here again, the French language makes a simple concept appear difficult.) Piaget's research suggests that the order of difficulty in learning conservation is: number, length, liquid quantity, mass, weight and volume.

Piaget found that number was the first attribute which children could learn to conserve. Even two year olds can begin to gain some simple understanding of number. They can usually say, "one, two . . ." and will hold up two fingers to indicate their age. Please note, however, that this action does not mean that a two year old has actually "internalized" the concept of "two" — rather that the earliest beginnings of number concepts are occurring. Some three and four year olds will begin to count to ten. Often, however, they will not count in the correct sequence. For example, the child may say, "1,2,3,4,6,8,5,10." Nursery school children can usually master simple problems of one-to-one correspondence. Teachers can give children experience in this area by having youngsters help to "set up" for juice. For example, each child needs one glass, one cracker, one napkin, one placemat, etc. Tasks 5 and 6 — at the end of this chapter can aid the teacher in determining the child's ability to conserve number.

Children need many experiences to learn to internalize the concept of numbers. The young child at play may casually count a row of blocks and discover there are five. He may stack them and again determine there are five. The child may then rearrange the blocks and, upon counting, discover that five still remain. In performing these operations, the child makes an important discovery related to the invariance of number.

Weight and volume are the last areas which the child learns to conserve. Task 12, presented at the end of this chapter, deals with volume. In this task two pieces of clay are placed in identical glasses of water. Then the examiner changes the shape of one piece of clay to a "hot dog." She then asks the youngster if the longer piece of clay will displace the same amount of water. The child who is unable to conserve believes the hot dog will displace more water. The conserving child recognizes that both pieces will displace equal amounts of water, regardless of shape.

Note: The protocol in Appendix A does not include a task for the conservation of weight. However, if the teacher has a set of balance scales she may wish to construct a task for this concept. The procedure is similar to the task for quantity (Task 3) and for volume (Task 12). Show the child two identical balls of clay and place them on the scales. Have the child confirm that both balls are the same. Roll one ball into the shape of a hot dog. Ask the child what will happen when both pieces are placed on the balance scales. The conserving child will recognize that the weight is the same despite the alternation in appearance.

Piaget believed children learned conservation as a result of maturation and via experiences. Children appear to learn conservation by engaging in activities which provide a wide variety of experiences in counting, measuring and comparing in order to "internalize" the concepts of number, weight, mass, volume, etc. Children can learn to count "by rote" — and this task is necessary for learning to enumerate; however, practice through play and related activities is necessary if one is to master the true meaning of number concepts.

Piaget did not believe that logic could be taught — at least not through verbal instruction. Some researchers have questioned this idea and have suggested that children can learn to conserve through the acquisition of certain verbal rules. Some investigators (Roeper & Sigel, 1967; Gelman,

1969; Weikart, 1971) have demonstrated that children can be helped to develop number logic and conservation skills through instruction and the utilization of concrete materials. Roeper and Sigel (1967) did a study in which children were given training in conservation. Gelman (1969) taught five year olds to conserve number and length by training children to focus (center) upon the relevant cues and appropriate relationships pursuant to the mastery of the task. Thus, it is suggested that through knowledge of the child's abilities and through diagnostic appraisal, the teacher can plan concrete experiences which will aid in understanding crucial concepts and in facilitating the learning process.

A problem in spatial relations

The youngsters will concentrate on "emptying the pitcher," rather than "filling the glass."

TASK 1: CONSERVATION OF LENGTH

Materials:

Two rods or sticks approximately four inches long and one-half inch in width. (Suggestion: Use Cuisenaire rods.)

Situation:

Have the subject line up the two rods along side each other. Ask, ARE THE RODS (STICKS) THE SAME LENGTH?

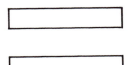

After the subject agrees that the rods are the same length, the examiner moves one of the rods about one inch ahead of the other rod. Ask, ARE THE RODS THE SAME LENGTH? If the child responds in the affirmative, ask, ARE YOU SURE? Shift the rods in a different direction. Ask, ARE THE RODS THE SAME LENGTH?

Requestioning:

Ask, TELL ME WHY YOU SAY THAT? If response is not adequate, probe further. For example: TELL ME MORE or HOW DO YOU KNOW? or ARE YOU SURE?

Appraisal:

UC   Subject conserved length. (Agreed rods remained the same length.) Score item UC — understands concept.

T   Subject conserved length on trial one; did not on trial two. Score item T — in transition. See comment below.

NH   Subject did not conserve length. (Said one rod was longer than the other.) Score item NH — need help.

Comment:

If the subject is two to four years old he will usually fail to understand this concept. Usually he will *center* on the length of the rod which was pushed forward and it will "appear" longer and he will not conserve. Note: The idea of "centering" is central to conservation. The preoperational child fails to conserve because he concentrates ("centers") on a narrow portion of the information which is available to him.

If subject answered differently when shift of rods was reversed, this may indicate that the subject is: 1) in a transition period related to conservation of length, or 2) lateral development is not equal. It is also possible that visual perception may be a problem. If, over a period of time, the subject continues to answer in the same manner with the same reasoning — further testing by a qualified examiner may be indicated. (Note: If child does not conserve in other areas, the problem is probably maturational, rather than perceptual.)

TASK 2: CONSERVATION OF DISTANCE

Materials:
  Two small blocks (one inch cubes).
  A book to use as divider.
  Construction paper — 8½" x 11".

Situation:
  On construction paper place two blocks in front of subject about one inch apart. Say, SEE THE TWO BLOCKS ON THIS PAPER, THEY ARE CLOSE TO EACH OTHER. MOVE THEM SO THEY ARE FAR APART.
  When the subject moves the blocks far apart, say, TELL ME WHAT YOU DID. After the child explains his action place the book between the two blocks and ask, ARE THE BLOCKS FAR APART OR ARE THEY CLOSE TO-GETHER?

Requestioning:
  TELL ME WHY YOU SAY THAT? If response is not adequate, probe further. For example: TELL ME MORE, or HOW DO YOU KNOW? or ARE YOU SURE?

Appraisal:
  UC   Subject conserved distance — said blocks were still far apart.
   T   Subject vacillated answer upon requestioning.
  NH   Subject did not conserve distance — said blocks were closer together.

Comment:
  Refer to comments in Task 1.

TASK 3: CONSERVATION OF QUANTITY

Materials:

Two balls of clay or play dough.

Situation:

Give the subject two balls of clay or play dough. Ask, ARE THE BALLS OF CLAY EXACTLY THE SAME? If the subject is not satisfied that they are the same, say, MAKE THEM EXACTLY THE SAME. Again ask if they are the same and be sure to have agreement before continuing. The examiner may need to assist if there is difficulty manipulating the material. Take *one* ball and roll it into a "hot dog." Ask, IS THERE AS MUCH CLAY HERE (point to the hot dog) AS THERE IS HERE? (point to the ball). Ask, DOES ONE PIECE HAVE MORE THAN THE OTHER?

Requestioning:

TELL ME WHY YOU SAY THAT? If response is not adequate or answers tend to be unsure, probe further. For example: TELL ME MORE or HOW DO YOU KNOW? or ARE YOU SURE?

Appraisal:

UC   Subject conserved quantity. Said there was still the same amount in each.

T   Subject vacillated answer upon requestioning.

NH   Subject did not conserve quantity. Said one piece had more than the other.

Comment:

Refer to earlier section in the chapter for a discussion of this task.

TASK 4: CONSERVATION OF AREA

Materials:
Two sheets of green construction paper (8½″ x 11″) to use as grassy pastures.
Two small plastic animals (cows or horses).
28 one inch blocks or counting cubicles.

Situation:
Place both pastures side by side, with approximately two inches between them and the 8½″ side, facing the child. Place a cow on each pasture. (Note: Plastic animals may be obtained in most dime stores. If these are not available, the examiner may use a picture of a horse or a cow.) Ask, DO BOTH COWS HAVE THE SAME AMOUNT OF GRASS TO EAT? Be sure to have agreement before further questioning. Place one house (block) on pasture A. Say, IN THIS PASTURE THE FARMER BUILT A HOUSE. Explain, WHEN THE FARMER BUILT THE HOUSE HE TOOK SOME OF THE GRASS OUT OF THE PASTURE. Ask, DO BOTH COWS HAVE THE SAME AMOUNT OF GRASS TO EAT?

If the subject says the cow in pasture A has less to eat, ask, WHAT DO WE NEED TO DO SO THAT BOTH COWS HAVE THE SAME AMOUNT TO EAT? The solution should be to place a house on pasture B. It may be necessary to relate the solution to the child and place the house on pasture B. Note: Place houses on pasture B in random order and scattered over the page. (See illustration in Appendix B.)

Ask, DO BOTH COWS NOW HAVE THE SAME AMOUNT OF GRASS TO EAT? Do not continue unless agreement is made that both pastures are the same.

Say, EACH TIME I PUT A HOUSE ON PASTURE A (point to the pasture), I WILL PLACE A HOUSE ON PASTURE B. (Point to pasture B.) Note in the illustration in Appendix B that the houses in pasture A are placed *in a row,* very close together and the houses in pasture B are *scattered* over the entire pasture.

After three houses have been placed in each field ask, DO BOTH COWS HAVE THE SAME AMOUNT OF GRASS TO EAT? Then ask, IS THERE ONE COW THAT HAS MORE GRASS TO EAT? If the child states that one field has more grass, ask him to clarify his statement and show you which pasture has the most grass.

Requestioning:

TELL ME WHY YOU SAY THAT? If the response is not adequate or the answers tend to lack clarity, probe further until the subject's response is understood. For example, ARE YOU SURE? WHY DO YOU THINK THAT? or HOW DO YOU KNOW? or TELL ME MORE.

Continuation of situation:

The same technique is used for five houses on each pasture; then seven, ten, and fourteen houses. In pasture A there are finally two rows of seven houses, close together. On pasture B the houses should be scattered over the page.

Appraisal:

Note: On the protocol, indicate the highest level of house area conserved. Thus: "one house area conserved" or "3 houses conserved" or "5 houses conserved" "7 houses conserved" or "10 houses conserved."

UC   Subject completely mastered the task. Conserved area with fourteen (14) houses.

T   Subject did not conserve area. The visual area was "overwhelming." (Example: Subject may conserve five or seven houses, but finally "gives in" to the optical illusion as more houses are added.)

NH   Subject did not conserve area after three or more houses were added.

Comment:

Continue to requestion until the child can no longer conserve. If he is able to conserve each situation, ask, IT LOOKS LIKE PASTURE A HAS LOTS MORE GRASS FOR ITS COW THAN PASTURE B . . . ARE YOU SURE

THEY HAVE THE SAME? If there is a slight uncertainty, continue to requestion until the subject's answer is definite. This is often where a child is found to be in transition from one stage to another. The best technique to discover the level of conceptualization is requestioning.

TASK 5: CONSERVATION OF NUMBER:
ONE-TO-ONE CORRESPONDENCE
(as many as)

Materials:
One set of seven circles.
One set of seven squares.

Situation:
(Note: This task is divided into *two* parts.) Place seven circles and seven squares before the subject. Place the objects in one-to-one correspondence. Ask, DO WE HAVE AS MANY CIRCLES AS WE HAVE SQUARES? Ask, HOW DO YOU KNOW? or TELL ME MORE.

Appraisal: (Part a)
UC Subject could do one-to-one correspondence. Agreed that there were the same number of circles and squares.
T Subject vacillated upon requestioning.
NH Subject did not conserve number — "as many as."

Continuation of Situation:
If the child establishes that the two sets are equivalent, push the circles in a smaller row (bunch them together) and spread the squares out in a second row. Ask, ARE THERE AS MANY CIRCLES AS THERE ARE SQUARES? Ask, HOW DO YOU KNOW?

Appraisal: (Part b)
UC Subject could conserve when circles were bunched.
T Subject vacillated upon requestioning.
NH Subject failed to conserve when circles were bunched.

Comment:
In the first part of this problem the examiner should determine if the child can perform the task of simple one-to-one correspondence. When the examiner "bunches" the

65

circles together the overall perception of the object is altered. If the child centers on the length of the row, he does not understand the invariance of number. When the rows differ in length he believes the longer line has the greatest number. The child may vacillate — he may handle one-to-one correspondence but cannot conserve the equivalence of a set when rearranged. If the examiner believes the child is in transition, she can regroup the sets in a different arrangement and see if the child can then conserve. If the examiner questions carefully, this task can provide insight into the child's level of conservation.

TASK 6: CONSERVATION OF NUMBER:
ONE-TO-ONE CORRESPONDENCE
(More than: Less than)

Materials:
  Set of five circles.
  Set of four squares.

Situation:
  (Note: Task 6 is divided into *three* parts and should be recorded as appropriate.) Give the five circles and four squares to the child. Say, TELL ME IF THERE ARE AS MANY SQUARES AS THERE ARE CIRCLES? After the child matches one-to-one (the circles to the squares), ask, WHICH SET HAS MORE? Next ask, WHICH SET HAS LESS? If vocabulary appears to be a problem, rephrase the questions and ask in another way.

Requestioning:
  Ask, TELL ME WHY YOU SAY THAT? If the subject did not provide sufficient information to determine positively — requestion and probe further. It may be necessary to ask for more explanation by saying, CAN YOU EXPLAIN FURTHER? ARE YOU SURE? WHY DO YOU THINK THAT? or HOW DO YOU KNOW?

Appraisal:

a)   UC   Subject could do one-to-one correspondence. Could conserve "as many as."

   T   Subject vacillated answer upon requestioning.

   NH   Subject did not conserve one-to-one.

b)   UC   Subject conserved number by identifying set with more.

   T   Subject vacillated answer upon requestioning.

	NH	Subject failed to identify set with more.
c)	UC	Subject conserved number by identifying set with less.
	T	Subject vacillated answer upon requestioning.
	NH	Subject failed to identify set with less.

Comment:
See comments in Task 7.

TASK: 7: CONSERVATION OF NUMBER: NUMBER AND SPACE

Materials:

Set of 14 buttons, seven one color and seven in contrasting color.

A bowl or other container. (Suggestion: Chips may be substituted.)

Situation:

Let the subject choose one set of buttons and have him place the buttons in a row on the table. The examiner takes the remaining set of buttons and places them in a row opposite the subject's buttons — in a 1:1 correspondence position. Say, ARE THERE THE SAME NUMBER OF BUTTONS IN MY ROW AS IN YOUR ROW? If the subject is able to agree, respace the buttons in the examiner's row so that the row is now obviously longer than the child's row of buttons. (See illustration below.)

Say, TELL ME, ARE THERE AS MANY BUTTONS IN YOUR ROW AS THERE ARE IN MY ROW?

Requestioning:

After listening to the child's answer and explanation, requestion. Say, ARE THERE MORE BUTTONS IN MY ROW OR MORE BUTTONS IN YOUR ROW? It may be necessary to ask for more explanation by saying, ARE YOU SURE? WHY DO YOU THINK THAT? or HOW DO YOU KNOW? or TELL ME MORE.

Appraisal:

UC   Subject conserved. Said there were the same number.

T   Subject vacillated upon requestioning.

NH   Subject did not conserve. Said one row had more buttons.

Comment:

If the child fails to accomplish this task it is because he *centers* on the length of the rows and bases his answer on this information only. When the rows are of different lengths, the non-conserver believes the longest line has the greatest number. If the child did not conserve, his logic is based on his own perceptions and he does not yet have the mathematical concept of number. He may be able to count to ten or even higher, but if he does not understand and *truly comprehend* number, he is *not* ready for the regimentation of addition and subtraction with abstract symbols. The child's ability to conserve is directly related to his understanding of more than, less than, and the invariance of number. He must be able to comprehend that the numeral "seven" stands for seven objects and these seven objects may be rearranged in any combination and there will still be seven. (For example, he must understand that 5 + 2; 3 + 4; 1 + 6 — all equal "seven" — and that this is the same as the numeral, "seven.")

TASK 8: CONSERVATION OF NUMBER: COUNTING

Materials:

Seven counting chips, buttons, or beads.

Situation:

Spread seven chips in front of the subject. Say, COUNT THE CHIPS IN FRONT OF YOU.

Requestioning:

Say, TELL ME HOW MANY CHIPS ARE HERE? Be sure to note the technique used by the child to count the chips. Did the subject look at the set and identify the number or did the child count one by one? Was he decisive in his technique? Did he count without making an error on the first trial?

Appraisal:

UC   Subject counted seven chips correctly.

  T   Counted orderly but did not know the actual cardinal number.

NH   Subject was unable to count the seven chips correctly.

Comment:

See comments in Task 7. At this stage of development, some children can successfully count objects in order, assign a number to each object and yet not really understand the final number. In order to determine the child's ability to count correctly, the examiner must pay strict attention to the child's technique and his comments. In some cases the subject may not actually realize that the final number recited is, *in fact*, the answer to the question, "How many." It is also possible for a subject to successfully count the chips and then tell the examiner that there are only three or four chips. It is also possible for the child to miscount and yet arrive at the correct answer. It is advisable to ask the child to count aloud.

TASK 9: CONSERVATION OF NUMBER: COUNTING BY REGROUPING

Materials:

Seven counting chips. (Same as Task 8).

Situation:

When the examiner has determined the subject knows there are seven chips in front of him, rearrange the chips in a divided or scattered position and ask, HOW MANY CHIPS ARE THERE NOW?

If the child begins to count the chips, seems unsure, hesitates or gives an incorrect response; he does not understand the invariance of number.

Requestioning:

If the examiner is unsure of the subject's response — requestion. It may be necessary to change the amount in the set and start over again.

Appraisal:

UC Subject gave correct answer when the set was regrouped without counting. Understood the invarianc of number.

 T Subject gave correct answer when set was regrouped by counting. Under these circumstances, the child does not understand the invariance of number.

NH Subject gave an incorrect answer.

Comment:

If the subject must count to determine the answer on each trial, the examiner can assume the child is beginning to comprehend the concept — but is in transition, and does not fully understand conservation of number. It is advisable to ask the child to count aloud.

TASK 10: CONSERVATION OF NUMBER:
ADDITIVE RELATIONS
(Parts to the whole.)

Materials:
Cheerios, Trix — or two cereals of different color.

Situation:
Say, LET'S PRETEND THESE CHEERIOS ARE FOR YOUR BREAKFAST AND LUNCH TODAY. I AM GOING TO DIVIDE THEM EQUALLY AND MAKE ONE ROW FOR BREAKFAST AND ONE ROW FOR LUNCH. (Place four Cheerios in a row — and 4 Cheerios in a second row.) Say, ARE THE TWO ROWS THE SAME? (Subject must agree before continuing.) NOW I AM GOING TO GIVE YOU SOME TRIX FOR TOMORROW. (Place four Trix in one row; 4 in another.) Ask ARE THE TWO ROWS THE SAME? (Subject must agree before continuing.) Say, BUT LET'S PRETEND THAT TOMOROW MORNING AT BREAKFAST YOU ARE *SO HUNGRY* THAT YOU EAT THIS MANY! (Move 3 Trix from the lunch group to the breakfast group — making seven in the breakfast group and only one remaining in the lunch group.) Ask, IS THERE THE SAME AMOUNT OF CEREAL FOR BOTH DAYS? If the child says no or seems confused say, IS THIS (point to Day 1: 4 + 4) THE SAME AS THIS GROUP? (Point to Day 2: 7 + 1.)

Requestioning:
If the child says no, move Day 2 back to 4 + 4 and ask, ARE THEY THE SAME NOW? WHY DO YOU SAY THAT? Move Day 2 back to 7 + 1 and ask, ARE THEY THE SAME NOW? TELL ME MORE. HOW DO YOU KNOW?

Appraisal:
  UC   Subject recognized that Day 1 and Day 2 were the same.
  T   Subject vacillated upon requestioning.

NH   Subject believed that Day 2 had more cereal or that there was more food for breakfast. Subject was confused.

Comment:

This task deals with the ability to recognize the invariance of number. Young children do not perceive a number as a constant totality which remains the same regardless of the arrangement of the parts.

TASK 11: MEASUREMENT OF HEIGHT

Materials:

Blocks of many different shapes and sizes.
Low table and adult chair.
Various measuring tools such as rulers, yard or meter stick, etc.

Situation:

Show the subject a tower of blocks on the chair. Say, BUILD A TOWER THE SAME HEIGHT AS MINE ON THE TABLE. The examiner should have the measuring instruments clearly in the view of the child, but should *not* make suggestions for their use.

Requestioning:

Closely observe the way in which the child approaches the task. If appropriate, ask, WHAT ARE YOU DOING?

Appraisal:

UC Subject was able to build tower exact height of the model using measuring instrument.

T Subject was able to build tower exact height using "line of sight" or body.

NH Subject was unable to construct tower of exact height of model.

Comment:

In this task it is actually more important to note the method used to build the tower and the method of thinking utilized by the youngster. The examiner should note where the subject appears on the continuum of development related to measurement of height.

Younger children would be expected to build a tower on the same visual level without worrying about the difference in the level of the table or the chair. They compare by stepping back to observe if the towers are the same height. A slightly older child may use a stick or rod to lay across the two towers to make sure they are level. Later in development the child notices that the base line of his tower is not at the same level as the model. He then begins to look for another measuring tool. One of the first tools utilized will be the child's own body and he may use the spread of his hands to make the comparison. Later children may resort to using reference points on the body such as the length of the arm or shoulder to the waist or some other referent part on the body.

Eventually the child will resort to measuring with an independent device such as a rod or stick. In the beginning the rod must be of the same length but later the child recognizes that it does not have to be so. He then discovers he may even use a shorter rod several times to measure the height.

The final discovery involves logical operations. The first operation allows the child to see the whole tower is composed of a number of parts (blocks) added together. The second operation allows the child to apply substitution and build on a system of units. Measurement develops later than the number concept because it is more difficult to divide a continuous whole into units so that it becomes measurable.

TASK 12: CONSERVATION OF VOLUME

Materials:
  Two balls of clay. (Same as Task 3.)
  Two glasses or beakers.

Situation:
  (Suggestion: For convenience you may wish to present this task immediately after completing Task 3.) Give the subject two balls of clay or play dough. Ask, ARE THE BALLS OF CLAY EXACTLY THE SAME? If the subject is not satisfied that they are the same, say, MAKE THEM EXACTLY THE SAME. Again ask if they are the same and be sure to have agreement before continuing. Fill the two beakers half-full with water. Have the child place the balls into the water and observe that they displace equal amounts of the liquid. Ask, CAN YOU SEE THAT THE TWO BALLS DISPLACE THE SAME AMOUNT OF WATER? (Note: Some young children will have difficulty with the term, displacement. The examiner may wish to change her wording. For example, DO YOU SEE THAT THE WATER IS *JUST AS HIGH* IN BOTH GLASSES? DO YOU SEE THAT THE WATER IS THE SAME? HOW? Be sure you have agreement before continuing.
  Take *one* ball and roll it into a "hot dog." Ask, WHICH OBJECT WILL DISPLACE MORE WATER? (Wait for a reply.) After the child responds, allow the child to again place both objects into the beakers. Ask, WHICH OBJECT DISPLACES MORE WATER?

Requestioning:
  Probe to determine how the child arrives at his answer: (a) *Before* the objects are placed in the beaker or (b) *after* the objects have been placed in the beaker. Ask, TELL ME MORE? WHAT HAS HAPPENED? ARE YOU SURE?

Appraisal:

UC Subject said both pieces would displace equal amounts of water *before* objects were placed in the beakers.

T Subject recognized that objects displaced the same amount of water, *after* objects had been placed in the beaker.

NH Subject said the "hot dog" displaced more water.

Comment:

Refer to the earlier discussion of conservation of quantity in the chapter. The length of the "hot dog" is overpowering to the preconserving child and he believes the "hot dog" has more clay. Likewise, the preconserving child will say that the hot dog will displace more water. When the child is in transition he will vacillate in his response. This vacillation will usually occur if the examiner probes the subject on his response. He will change his mind and finally appear very confused. The conserving child recognizes that the transformation is visual and will say that both pieces displace the same amount of water.

CHAPTER FOUR

Classification

One basic prerequisite for abstract thinking is the ability to classify. Initially the child is unable to devise any significant criteria for classification. During the sensori-motor phase there appears to be a primitive type of motoric classification. Piaget calls this type of activity the abbreviation of a schema which is known to the child. For example, a bottle is something to suck; a rattle is something to shake. One can see that this mode of thinking is actually not true classification since the schema refers to one object. In true classification there is the recognition that a group of objects belong to an even larger grouping. For example, "All of these pencils are sharpened," or "all the blocks in this box are wooden."

Piaget identified three stages of classification in children between the ages of two to eleven years. Stage one occurs between the ages of two to four years. Near the end of the sensori-motor period, the youngster may begin to classify, but often the classification will be based on incorrect observations or assumptions. For example: All women are mothers; all women teachers are mothers; all men teachers are fathers. Or a child may view the family dog as his brother because the dog lives in the same house as he does. In the second stage, ages five to seven years, the youngster begins to sort in a logical manner and uses some reasonable criteria which is recognizable. In stage two, the child can use some preconceived plan for the purpose of classifying objects. During this stage the more advanced child begins to make hierarchies in classification. In stage three (7-11 years of age), the child can make hierarchies which are more complicated. As the child becomes older and more mature he will ultimately be able to classify objects which are not physically present — for example, "dogs and cats are animals" or "all the states comprise the United States." In stage three the child is capable of understanding class inclusion. This stage, class inclusion, is the highest level of classification and represents the ability to comprehend the parts and the whole simultaneously.

Graphic Collections and Chaining. (Stage One)

At two to four years there are two types of pre-classification behavior: graphic collections and chaining.

In graphic collections one will observe the child grouping items together for no apparent reason other than, "They just go together!" Piaget also uses the term "partial alignment" to describe this activity. The child uses some of the objects to make the grouping — but there is no obvious plan or strategy. In this stage, if a child is given a wide variety of small toys and told to group them in some fashion, he may place two toy autos together and then add a toy bus and a truck to the collection. However, upon questioning the child, one usually finds that the youngster "seems to know" that similar characteristics exist, even though he does not fully comprehend the qualities of the class he has created.

In chaining the child places items in a line (or chain) rather than groups. During chaining the child may verbalize: "The truck goes with the block because they are both wood. The block goes with the ball because they are both red. The fire engine goes with the red ball because they both roll," etc. During this period if a child is given a group of geometric forms he may place green squares in a row ("because they are alike"). However, when he runs out of green squares he adds green circles to the group ("because they are green"). He may continue his chain by adding blue and red circles ("because they are circles"). The child, at this stage, is able to focus on only one attribute. Then, forgetting his original criterion, he changes to a new one. Thus each decision determines the subsequent one rather than some preconceived plan for grouping the items.

When classifying by "chaining" the young child initially focuses on a single attribute. Then, forgetting his original criterion, he begins anew.

Classifying in a Logical Manner. (Stage Two)

At five to seven years, children begin to form classes based on some recognizable criteria. For example: members of a class are similar; the defining property of a class determines the objects which will fit the class, etc.

Piaget constructed an experiment using squares, triangles, circles and half-circles, which were all the same color. After placing them before the child he said, "Put things together that are alike" or "Put the objects in a pile which look alike." Given this task the younger children (2-4 years), would include *some* of the items in an array (*partial alignment*); other youngsters would "chain" the objects. Older children (5-7) began to make collections which could be labeled true classes. Piaget found that initially older children made four piles: squares, triangles, circles and half-circles. (Note the older children did not "chain" — rather their classes had the attribute of similarity and they utilized *all* the objects for the classification task.) Piaget also noted that more advanced youngsters would create a hierarchy. These children indicated that circles and half-circles formed a larger class (a supraclass) of "curved forms." They also placed the squares and triangles into a larger class of "angular forms" or polygons. The reader may wish to try this experiment with children in addition to the suggested classification tasks which are listed at the end of the chapter.

When children begin to classify in a logical manner their initial attempts are usually small groupings rather than supragroupings. For example, if a child is presented with a

number of red and yellow pencils, some long, some short, some sharpened, some not, he may group as follows:
   All short, red sharpened pencils
   All short, yellow, sharpened pencils
   All short, red unsharpened pencils
   All short, yellow unsharpened pencils
   All long, yellow sharpened pencils
   All long, red sharpened pencils
   All long, red unsharpened pencils
   All long, yellow, unsharpened pencils

When a child chooses this method of classification it indicates that he has progressed in logical development by noting that items are classed in terms of a simple classification scheme. It also indicates that the child has the ability to devise a preconceived plan and follow it through.

At a more advanced level the child may reduce his groupings (collapse the categories). For example:
   All short, sharpened pencils (red and yellow)
   All short, unsharpened pencils (red and yellow)
   All long, sharpened pencils (red and yellow)
   All long, unsharpened pencils (red and yellow)

Or some children may group as follows:

Short pencils (sharpened or unsharpened, red and yellow)
Long pencils (sharpened and unsharpened, red and yellow)

In the initial classification the child could classify items only when they were identical. In the more advanced stages the child can "override" one class (for example color or sharpened vs. unsharpened) and group into a hierarchical grouping or a supraclass.

When the child can *dichotomize* (classify into two major groups) it is obvious that he has incorporated several classificatory skills. He sees that items can be classed in terms of certain attributes and recognizes the similarity between apparently dissimilar objects. In these instances, however, he can override the dissimilarity and continue to classify according to his preconceived plan.

The nursery school and kindergarten teacher will recognize the difficulty the young child has in realizing that he can live in a neighborhood, a city, a county, a state and a nation at the same time. Or the child who cannot understand how the teacher can be a wife, mother, woman and teacher simultaneously.

To perform the above function the child must be able to shift criteria. In our example with the pencils the teacher would say, "I see you have put all the short pencils in one pile and all the long pencils in another. Now can you take *all* the pencils and sort them in another way?" In order to redivide the group the child must first get rid of his original "set" and search for a new criterion to serve as a basis for the resorting. If the child is able to perform the task it shows a recognition that an item can have several attributes and not belong exclusively to a single class.

Seriation.

Children become aware of similarities and differences at an early age. They recognize different sounds: they may smile at mother's voice and cry when a door slams. They learn functional differences: the infant quickly learns to shake toys that rattle and squeeze the toys that squeak.

The awareness that things are cognate; e.g., grouping items together on the basis of similar characteristics, is a prerequisite to classification. The same is true for the reverse — that is, the child must learn to recognize differences if he is to properly classify. Thus the ability to generalize and to differentiate helps to enhance the learning process. Two- and three-year-olds can be observed utilizing this concept in their free play. They systematically place new toys in one pile; old broken toys in another; blocks are stacked in one area; books are placed on a book shelf. The process of classification contributes to the understanding of *cardinal numbering*. (By cardinal numbering we mean a symbol which represents a class — not according

83

to the attributes of its members, but in terms of the number of its members.) Thus:

similarity ⟶ classification ⟶ cardination

Recognition of difference leads to seriation (big, bigger, biggest; tall, taller, tallest). Initially the child seriates by observing gross differences: big trike, little trike; big block, little block. Over time the child learns to make finer discriminations until it is possible to arrange a number of objects in ascending or descending order. Early experiences with seriation provide the logical structure needed to understand cardinal numbers. When a child seriates three objects in terms of size (big, bigger, biggest) he is involved in both seriation and ordination; that is, first, second and third in ordering. Thus:

difference ⟶ seriation ⟶ ordination

A typical seriation task would be to arrange several sticks or cylinders according to length. Most four to five year old children can successfully arrange a grouping with two to four elements. Some five to seven year olds can arrange four to ten elements — but only after a laborious procedure of trial and error. Usually the child cannot "operationally" arrange a series of eight to ten sticks (in ascending or descending order) until he is seven or eight years of age. By "operational," we mean that the child arranges the sticks by using some anticipatory scheme. Thus as the child arranges the sticks in ascending order, he logically reasons that each stick (as it is placed in sequence) must be the smallest of the remaining sticks. At the same time he realizes that his choice is longer than the stick previously chosen. Note that operational reasoning in seriation has its counterpart in classification, since both tasks require foresight and hindsight. When classifying, the child must remember his reason for grouping (hindsight) and project his criteria to subsequent items (foresight).

Class Inclusion. (Stage Three)

The highest level of classification is class inclusion. In class inclusion the child is capable of thinking of the whole and the parts simultaneously. He is able to *decenter* from the part and perceive the whole. He can construct a hierarchy and yet see the various relations within the grouping. Class inclusion is the process of combining subgroups (apples, peaches, and pears) into one supragroup (fruit). The process can also be reversed by separating the parts from the whole. Initially the teacher may feel that if she teaches the child that an apple and an orange are both fruit, she will have solved the problem of class inclusion.

Are there more apples or more fruit?

Young children will usually say, "more apples," because they are not able to combine the subclasses of apples, pears and peaches into one large supraclass (fruit).

Unfortunately the teacher is only dealing with a portion of classification and the child will not likely be able to organize this information into any meaningful whole-part structure. Again, unfortunately, the teacher may teach the concept by rote and mistakenly believe that the child has really internalized the idea. We are reminded of the mathematical concept which comedian Bill Cosby quotes in describing a kindergarten child:

"2 + 2 = 4"

"Man, that's great . . . 2 + 2 = 4"

"2 + 2 = 4 . . . that's really cool!!"

"Teacher, what's a two?"

Piaget conducted a relatively simple experiment in terms of class inclusion. He presented children with a box containing twenty wooden beads: eighteen brown beads and two white beads. Piaget asked children three to five-years-old, "Are there more brown beads or more wooden beads?" While the children understood that the beads were *all* wooden, and that some were brown and some were white, they still insisted that there were *more* brown beads. It would appear that the class of wooden beads was an *abstraction,* while the color of the beads (white & brown) was *concrete.* The child was unable to think of the parts and the whole simultaneously. In the section which follows, the task, Class Inclusion II, is similar to Piaget's experiment with the beads. However, for ease in administration, the task uses fewer objects (buttons). If desired, the reader may wish to substitute other items or even duplicate Piaget's actual experiment with beads.

When the child is able to internalize the idea of class inclusion he has attained a relatively high degree of cognitive skill. This stage of development does not occur at the preoperational level. Once attained, however, the child can construct a hierarchical system by combining several sub-classes to make a supraclass. He can also work the process in reverse. Thus, he can view the parts of the hierarchy while still retaining the image of the whole.

TASK 13: SIMPLE CLASSIFICATION

Materials:
Four long red pencils (2 sharpened).
Four short red pencils (2 sharpened).
Four long yellow pencils (2 sharpened).
Four short yellow pencils (2 sharpened).
Two boxes large enough to hold pencils.
See comment for alternate materials.

Situation:
Place pencils on the table in full view of the subject. Ask, WHAT DO YOU SEE? If the child does not respond with all the categories, hold two at a time in front of the subject and ask, HOW ARE THESE DIFFERENT?

If these questions do not produce the desired response, ask, ARE THESE TWO PENCILS THE SAME SIZE? COLOR? SHARPENED? The examiner should be sure that the subject recognizes each category. Then say, PUT TOGETHER THE PENCILS YOU THINK WILL GO TOGETHER.

Requestioning:
If the subject makes no response, probe further and repeat, PUT TOGETHER THOSE PENCILS THAT ARE ALIKE. HOW DID YOU KNOW TO PUT THE PENCILS TOGETHER THAT WAY?

Appraisal:
(Note: Task 13 is divided into four groups on the protocol and should be recorded, as appropriate.)

a)   UC   Subject made a graphic collection.
     NH   Subject unable to make a graphic collection.
b)   UC   Subject made a chain of objects.
     NH   Subject did not chain the objects.
c)   UC   Subject made eight groups of identical
                 objects.
     NH   Subject did not make eight groups.

d)   UC   Subject made four groups of identical objects.
       NH   Subject did not make four groups.

Comment:

If it is difficult to obtain sixteen pencils, there are other items which can be dichotomized. Items which are readily available include: nuts, seashells, buttons, nails, and screws. Our examiners have preferred pencils and buttons. One can usually locate large and small buttons, two and four hole buttons, and decorative and plain buttons in multiple colors.

Please note that the protocol has four parts for Task 13. These are recorded as UC (understands the concept) or NH (needs help). There is no transition category for Task 13.

If the subject dichotomized during simple classification, it can be assumed that the child understands the concepts of graphic collecting, chaining and grouping of four and eight identical objects. These categories (a,b,c,d) in Task 13 should be recorded as (UC), understands the concept, and the examiner can move on to Task 15. On some occasions the subject may voluntarily produce a first, second or third dichotomy during Task 13. In these instances, the examiner should record UC for Tasks 14, 15, and 16 and go on to Task 17.

Questioning the child on his rationale for classification can be most revealing in terms of understanding the child's mode of thinking and approach to the problem. Often the explanation provided will reveal how differently the child approaches a problem and how his mode of thinking is, in fact, different from the adult. The way in which the child dichotomizes will provide the examiner insight into the subject's particular cognitive style. The examiner should be aware that during the early period of development that the child may dichotomize and yet be unable to explain his rationale for grouping as he classifies.

88

TASK 14 CLASSIFICATION: FIRST DICHOTOMY

Note: If the child made a dichotomy in Task 13, it is not necessary to present this situation to the child.

Materials:
Same as in Task 13.

Situation:
Mix all the pencils together and place the two boxes in front of the subject. Say, PUT ALL OF THE PEN-CILS INTO TWO BUNDLES. BE SURE TO PUT PEN-CILS THAT GO TOGETHER IN SOME WAY. PLACE ONE GROUP OF PENCILS IN THIS BOX AND ONE GROUP IN THE OTHER BOX.

Requestioning:
Ask the subject to justify or explain how he arrived at his system of classification. Probe, if necessary, for a full explanation.

Appraisal:
UC Subject dichotomized. Record the method used: by color; by size; by sharpness.
NH Child was unable to dichotomize.

Comment:
Note that there is no transition category for Task 14. See additional comments in Task 13.

TASK 15: CLASSIFICATION: SECOND DICHOTOMY

Note: If the child has made a second dichotomy in either Task 13 or 14, this task is unnecessary.

Materials:
   Same as Task 13.

Situation:
   Review the first dichotomy with the subject. Say, NOW GROUP THE PENCILS IN A DIFFERENT WAY THAN THE LAST TIME BUT BE SURE TO PUT PENCILS TOGETHER THAT GO TOGETHER IN SOME WAY. PUT ONE GROUP IN THIS BOX AND THE OTHER GROUP IN THE OTHER BOX. If the subject repeats the first dichotomy, say, THAT'S FINE . . . NOW I WANT YOU TO THINK OF ANOTHER WAY TO MAKE TWO BUNDLES.

Requestioning:
   WHY DID YOU DECIDE TO PUT THE BUNDLES TOGETHER THAT WAY?

Appraisal:
   UC Subject dichotomized new way. Record method: by color; by size; by sharpness.
   NH Subject could not dichotomize in a new way.

Comment:
   Note that there is no transition category for Task 15. See additional comments in Task 13.

TASK 16: CLASSIFICATION: THIRD DICHOTOMY

Note: If the child has made a third dichotomy in Tasks 13, 14, or 15, Task 16 is unnecessary.

Materials:
    Same as Task 13.

Situation:
    Review the first and second dichotomy with the subject. Say, NOW GROUP THE PENCILS IN A DIFFERENT WAY THAN THE LAST TWO TIMES. PUT ONE GROUP OF PENCILS IN THIS BOX AND THE OTHER GROUP IN THE OTHER BOX. BE SURE THE PENCILS THAT GO TOGETHER ARE PLACED IN THE SAME BUNDLE. Follow the same procedure as in Task 14 if the child repeats an earlier dichotomy.

Requestioning:
    WHY DID YOU DECIDE TO PUT THE BUNDLES TOGETHER THAT WAY?

Appraisal:
    UC   Subject made third dichotomy. Record method: by color; by size; by sharpness.
    NH   Subject did not make the third dichotomy.

Comment:
    Note that there is no transition category for Task 16. See additional comments in Task 13.

TASK 17: SERIATION: STICKS

Materials:

Strip of masking tape (about 24″) placed horizonally on table in front of the child.

One set of ten sticks (¼″ to ½″ wide) cut from brown construction paper or cardboard. Each stick should vary in length by ½″ increments. Sticks should be the following lengths:

2″	2½″	3″	3½″	4″
4½″	5″	5½″	6″	6½″

One set of ten balloons cut from red construction paper. Balloons should vary in diameter in approximately ½″ increments. Diameters of balloons are:

½″	1″	1½″	2″	2½″
3″	3½″	4″	4½″	5″

Situation:

Say, HERE ARE TEN BROWN STICKS THAT ARE USED FOR BALLOONS. (Show the child one balloon.) PUT THE STICKS IN ORDER FROM THE SHORTEST TO THE LONGEST. PLACE EACH STICK ON THE BOTTOM OF THIS LINE. [Note: Point to the masking tape. If a straight edge is not used, children often forget (fail to conserve) to align the sticks.]

Requestioning:

WHY DID YOU LAY THE STICKS THIS WAY? If answer is short or inconclusive say, TELL ME MORE. I AM NOT QUITE SURE THAT I UNDERSTAND or TELL ME ANOTHER WAY or CAN YOU THINK OF ANOTHER WAY?

Appraisal:

UC   Subject seriated sticks systematically.

T Subject seriated sticks partially (made gross discriminations.)

NH Subject did not seriate all ten sticks.

Comment:

Children may be able to seriate but may not possess sufficient language facility to describe their actions. Asking the child sometimes provides further information and insight into their relational concepts, vocabulary development and thinking process.

The child who seriated both the sticks and balloons with ease would appear to have the logic of ordering on the concrete level. Before expecting the child to abstractly comprehend ordinal numbers he should be able to order and manipulate materials on the concrete level.

TASK 18: SERIATION: BALLOONS

Note: If subject failed to seriate all ten sticks in Task 17, do not administer Task 18.

Materials:
Use materials listed in Task 17.

Situation:
Say, PRETEND THESE RED CIRCLES ARE BALLOONS. PLACE ONE BALLOON OVER EACH STICK, BUT NOT TOUCHING THE STICK. BE SURE THAT THE SMALLEST BALLOON GOES WITH THE SHORTEST STICK AND THE LARGEST BALLOON GOES WITH THE LONGEST STICK. The examiner should be sure that the sticks are sufficiently separated for the balloons to fit properly in their respective places.

Requestioning:
WHY DID YOU PLACE THEM THAT WAY? TELL ME IN ANOTHER WAY WHY YOU DECIDED TO PLACE THE BALLOONS THAT WAY.

Appraisal:
- UC Subject seriated balloons systematically and correctly.
- T Subject seriated balloons partially (made gross discriminations.)
- NH Subject did not seriate all ten balloons.

Comment:
Refer to the section on seriation in the chapter. In addition, see comments in Task 17.

TASK 19: CLASS INCLUSION I

Materials:
   Five plastic animals (four dogs and one cat).

Situation:
   Place the animals on the table before the child. Say, SOME OF THE ANIMALS ARE DOGS (separate the dogs into one area) AND ONE ANIMAL IS A CAT.
   While pointing to the dogs ask, ARE ALL OF THESE ANIMALS DOGS? While pointing to the cat ask, IS THIS ANIMAL A CAT? The child must provide the correct responses before continuing with the task. Then ask, ARE THERE MORE DOGS HERE OR MORE ANIMALS?

Requestioning:
   WHY DO YOU SAY THERE ARE MORE_____? ARE YOU SURE? Sometimes children are confused by the language. If this appears to be the case, return all the animals to the table. Say, ARE ALL THE ANIMALS DOGS? Say, NOW LISTEN CAREFULLY, IF YOU TOOK SOME OF THE DOGS AWAY, WOULD THERE BE ANY DOGS LEFT? Then, IF YOU TOOK ALL OF THE DOGS AWAY WOULD THERE BE ANY ANIMALS LEFT? Then ask the child, ARE THERE MORE DOGS OR MORE ANIMALS? (Pause) ARE YOU SURE? If the child answers correctly on the initial question but then tends to "flip flop" his answers upon requestioning, this indecision is an indication of transition.

Appraisal:
   UC Subject understood class inclusion — said more animals.
   T Subject vacillated upon requestioning.
   NH Subject did not understand class inclusion — said more dogs.

Comment:

Refer to the discussion on class inclusion in the earlier section of this chapter. The child who answers "more animals" would appear to understand class inclusion. He has the ability to conceive the whole and its parts at the same time without losing the image of either set.

The child who answers "more dogs" knows that the dogs are part of the whole of animals and that there are dog animals and cat animals. The difficulty comes when the youngster must think of the whole and its parts simultaneously. He must be able to *decenter* the part and perceive the whole. If the child scores NH on this task, it is not necessary to administer Task 20.

TASK 20: CLASS INCLUSION II

Materials:
  Ten yellow plastic buttons.
  Two red plastic buttons.
  (Suggestion: Use two kinds of cereal like Cheerios & Trix.)

Situation:
  Place the buttons before the child. Ask generalized questions that require the child to recognize the characteristics which make up this set of buttons — color: red, yellow; material: plastic. Say, TELL ME ABOUT THESE BUTTONS. HOW ARE THEY THE SAME? HOW ARE THE BUTTONS DIFFERENT? WHAT ARE THESE BUTTONS MADE OF? After all descriptions have been made clear to the child and he understands their color and their material, ask, ARE THERE MORE YELLOW BUTTONS OR MORE PLASTIC BUTTONS? or WHICH WOULD MAKE A BIGGER GROUP — ALL THE YELLOW BUTTONS OR ALL THE PLASTIC BUTTONS?

Requestioning:
  HOW DO YOU KNOW THERE ARE MORE? WHY DO YOU SAY THAT?

Appraisal:
  UC Subject said more plastic buttons. Understood class inclusion.
  T Subject vacillated answer upon requestioning.
  NH Subject said more yellow buttons. Could not deal with class inclusion or compare part to the whole.

Comment:
  This task may be more difficult than Task 19 because there are more objects involved and the child must *really*

concentrate to think in terms of both the parts and the whole simultaneously. When he is capable of class inclusion, the child will usually respond by saying, "The biggest group of buttons would be the plastic buttons because you would have *all* the yellow ones as well!" While the child can separate the colors (red and yellow), he must also perceive that there is a greater whole — buttons.

CHAPTER FIVE

Temporal Relations

Temporal relations deals with the aspect of time. It is concerned with the way the child interprets his environment when he is asked to recall past events, anticipate, predict, plan, and understand how events are related to one another in time. Eventually he must attain mastery of conventional systems and methods which are used to measure time.

Young children's concepts of time are quite different than that of an adult. If you have ever tried to explain when Santa Claus will come, when it will be time for a favorite TV show, when it will be time for a child's birthday party, or when grandmother is coming; you recognize that children do not comprehend the adult time system. When the early childhood educator attempts to respond to the child by using "adult time," she is seldom understood. Answers such as "fortnight," "a long time away," "soon," "not for a long time," "in a few minutes," or "next week" have little meaning. In fact, there are instances when the preschool child will immediately respond to the teacher and say something like, "Is it tomorrow now?"

Young children do not understand the adult method of measuring time in minutes, hours, days, weeks, months, seasons, years, decades, and centuries. In addition, instruments used to measure time — like the calendar or a clock, have little meaning for children until they have mastered a basic understanding of time. Basic concepts about time help children learn to master standard units of time and instruments for measurement. Much later these concepts will help youngsters relate to and comprehend changes and cause and effect in fields such as history and science.

Since young children are egocentric, they do not have an objective view of time. Time is understood only in terms of their own feelings. The movement of the clock hands has no connection with the passing of time for the young child. A short, dull conversation among adults would be considered a much longer period of time by a young child than an entire afternoon spent playing with his favorite toys. (The same situation is actually true for adults, but they recognize that it just *seems* longer!) The first experience which a child usually has with time is having to wait for something nice to happen. For an excited child a short period of waiting seems to be an eternity. For this reason it is wise not to spend weeks making preparations for special holidays like Christmas. If the school experience ends in early December, parents have a very excited child for almost an entire month plus an unhappy youngster while he is impatiently waiting. Then, the day after Christmas, one often hears the young child ask, "Mommy, when is Santa coming again? Will he be here tonight?"

Young children are usually unable to understand the quantitative measurement of time. This lack of ability is related to their understanding of the logic of number and the skills of subdividing a whole into its parts. Quantitative measurement is a concept which preoperational children generally cannot be expected to master. While a few children may begin to internalize these concepts, the amount of time expended is not worth the effort. Most young children do not have the conceptual ability to compare standard units, count the units and compare totals. Since it is not obvious or even understandable, it should not be an expected goal for an early childhood curriculum.

If all elementary school teachers were asked to evaluate children's ability to understand clocks and calendars, the major response would probably be that children do not learn these concepts easily. This reaction is not difficult to understand if one considers that clocks and calendars are abstract symbols which represent a concept (time) which cannot be directly observed. Thus, time is a relatively high level of abstraction and exists only in the mind.

"Mommy, will Santa come again tonight?"

As with other cognitive tasks such as number and space, the child must organize and adapt temporal concepts over a long period of cognitive development. It is actually not until the child reaches adolescence that he is fully capable of understanding and dealing with the total concept of time. Generally change theories, historical developments, and developmental trends are not presented until the child reaches a high school curriculum. In a study the authors found that some 12-14 year olds were unable to fully comprehend time concepts related to early historical periods. Thus, it is not surprising to find that most young children only superficially understand what the calendar represents.

Time and space as meaningful concepts are not separated for most children until the concrete operational period. The child in the preschool and primary grades cannot conceptualize the interrelationship of time, distance traveled, and speed (velocity) in his mind. He will tell you that the longer road (in distance) must take longer (in time) to travel than a shorter one, without considering the variable of speed. He simply thinks that the car that has moved for the longer time must have gone further than one which had been in motion for less time. He cannot understand how two objects, moving at different speeds, can start and stop at the same time. The child thinks the car moving more slowly *must* have stopped first. He compares the speed of two moving objects by observing whether one passes the other.

In one experiment, Piaget placed marbles on two inclines which differed in the angle of attack. In a second experiment children were shown two marbles of different sizes which were placed on the same incline. Piaget then "covered" the inclines with a tunnel and asked the children to predict which marble would emerge from the tunnel first? The children were unable to predict which marble was faster and which would be the first to roll out of the tunnel. (Note: We have not included these experiments in our set of tasks. However, they are easy for the teacher to prepare and administer, if she so desires.)

The child in the preoperational stage has other misconceptions regarding time and the labels given to time. Recurring events like "juice time," "lunch time," "math

102

time," "rest time," or "bed time" are seen as places which will not exist unless the child is physically present in the appropriate place. At this stage the child confuses age with size. The bigger the person, the older that individual is thought to be. Adults are often surprised when a pre-schooler may query, "Are you a hundred years old?"

"Yep, I'm older!"

The child in the preoperational stage has little ability to order events in a time frame or reconstruct the stages of any change process. The child usually cannot arrange cards in sequence which show a simple process like pouring water from one container to another. Sequencing represents the initial stages of learning the concept of order and seriation. The child must be able to seriate events before he can be expected to have the concept of reversibility and sequencing.

The young child cannot comprehend how one time interval can be included in a longer time interval. It is difficult to imagine how the morning can be a part of today and the youngster cannot easily respond to which event represents a longer time frame.

Educational Implications for Temporal Relations.

An early childhood educator must be aware of the "natural" limitations children have related to temporal relations. Once the teacher recognizes that the child's thinking process is totally different, it is obvious that expecting the child to comprehend a date like 1492 or an event like "The War of 1812," is beyond his ability. It is also inappropriate to expect the child to be able to "tell time" by the clock before he learns sequencing. He must recognize, "If event one happened before event two; event two occurred after event one." Prior to ordering events he must understand what "how old are you?" really means.

The early childhood educator should establish goals which are appropriate for the individual children with whom she is teaching. These goals should be based on daily contact and observation with the children. As the year progresses, goals for individual children should be adapted to the child's rate of development and learning.

The young child needs a regular classroom routine. The schedule must be talked about daily and should stay the same within limits so that the child develops security in knowing how his day will proceed. Once the teacher understands that the child really does not comprehend her "clock time" it is easy to see that the child tells time by what happens first, second and next. Once Piaget's daughter asked her father the name of the day. When Piaget answered, "Sunday," the child promptly told him it could not be Sunday because they had not gone to church.

Reversing the order of the day is also noticed as children become older. *A child tells time by what happens in the ordering of his day.* If you leave group time out one morning it may not be easy for the child to agree to go to lunch. Thus, if the teacher changes the order of the day she may be admonished and corrected. An excellent story to read to children which deals with reversing the order of the day is *The Backward Day* by Ruth Krauss. Once this story has been introduced, it is easier to say to the class "Today is a backward day." The children will then understand that the sequence of the day is reversed or is out of order. Putting coats on backwards may help children comprehend backwardness and order on special days. The teacher may be able to skip pages when reading a favorite story to a two-year-old but the four-year-old demands that every page be read in sequence. This awareness is the beginning of understanding sequence and temporal relations.

Several years ago one of the authors conducted an experiment with a group of three- and four-year-old children. Ordinarily this group met in the mornings for a three hour period (9 a.m. to noon). One day, with parent cooperation, the group meeting time was reduced fifty percent — from 9 a.m. to 10:30 a.m. During this shortened period the teacher and the assistants followed the regular schedule. However, snack time was at 9:30 (instead of 10:15); outdoor time was from 9:50 to 10:10 (instead of 11:00 to 11:40) and lunch was at 10:15 instead of 11:45. While the teacher and assistants were rushed and a bit harried, none of the children complained about the time reduction. None of the children mentioned the time difference during school hours or later with the parents.

As the teacher plans temporal experiences for the child, she should begin with active experiences which are supplemented and expanded by language experiences. The child needs concrete objects and actions before he will be ready for abstract stories and pictures. After the child understands a concept on the concrete level it may be extended to the semi-concrete level with pictures and actions. When teaching concepts related to the temporal area the child should be involved as much as possible. The child's surrounding environment and the routines should be incorporated into experiences to enhance learning the concept of time.

Language used to describe temporal concepts should relate to the activities of the day emphasizing the time of the day. Beginning and ending points should be labeled. A few minutes before it is time to go outside, the teacher should say, "five minutes until it is time to go outside" or "it is almost time to go outside; you need to begin to put your things away." Be sure that children become aware of time intervals. Help them to start activities, finish them, and understand the vocabulary of starting and stopping.

The teacher should also help children to order events of the day and incorporate terms like earlier, later, awhile ago, now, one more time, again, when, until, at the same time, then, before, during, after, since, and next. The teacher should also help children learn the relation of first, second, third, last or first, next and last. Children should be helped to understand what happens after lunch and before they go home for the day. The security of the schedule helps the child to sequence and order events. Children can also begin to label what happens in the morning and in the afternoon. For example, "In the morning we do group time or sharing first, music and then story. After lunch in the afternoon we have rest and then go outside, etc." This ordering represents the beginning of sequencing events and classifying the day in time frames.

Another way the teacher can help children become aware of temporal relations is to compare rates of movement or change using vocabulary of fast, slow, faster or slower. The expander vocabulary helps children to understand the concept of time (speedy, swift, quick, quicker, rapid, etc.) As children begin to understand the temporal vocabulary they will begin to compare time intervals. They recognize that a day is made of hours but may not be able to label the hours. Likewise, they may recognize that a week is composed of days and yet be unable to label the weekdays.

The child recognizes the term, "next day," as "After I go

to bed and sleep all night it will be the next day." A "week away" is going to bed seven times and getting up seven times. Seven days is a long time for some children and Christmas, a year away, is too much to count. The teacher should help children compare time periods by using "common sense aids" to help relate to the abstract concept of time.

Conventional units of time should be used in the teacher's vocabulary to assist the child in becoming familiar with temporal language. While children may begin to use time concepts in their everyday vocabulary, it takes a long time for the child to fully comprehend time frames. For example:

One day — day, night, today, tomorrow, the next day
Within a day — morning, afternoon, evening
Future — tomorrow, the next day, this weekend, a week from Tuesday
Past — last week, yesterday, the day before yesterday
Days of the week — Monday, Tuesday, Wednesday . . .
Comparison — school days vs. home days; holidays vs. Sundays
Dates — February 13, 1985
Units of time — a nanosecond, second, minute, half-hour, hour

It is the hope of the writers that teachers will utilize the tasks which follow to help them understand misconceptions which children may have regarding time. Teachers may also become aware that they have been too eager in teaching calendar vocabulary and telling time without full understanding on the part of the child. After the teacher has appraised the children's abilities in terms of temporal relations, the curriculum should be planned with specific goals. *Temporal relations are not taught in one lesson or one day.* It is a gradual process which takes place over the years. Children need many concrete experiences before they will be able to read and comprehend the calendar date or the meaning of clock hours.

TASK 21: TIME AND SPACE SEPARATION

Materials:

Two roads 36″ in length made of construction paper or masking tape. The roads should be placed parallel to each other, one on each side of a small table.

Two cars of different colors.

Situation:

Say, EACH OF US HAS A CAR AND EACH CAR HAS A ROAD TO DRIVE ON. YOU PLACE YOUR CAR HERE AT THE START OF YOUR ROAD, AND I WILL PUT MY CAR HERE (Place the examiner's car two to four inches in front of the subject's car.) Then say, WHEN YOU SAY "GO" WE WILL BOTH DRIVE OUR CARS TOWARD THE END OF THE ROADS. WHEN YOUR CAR GETS TO THE END OF YOUR ROAD SAY, "STOP" AND BOTH CARS WILL STOP. Be sure that the subject understands your directions and rephrase, if necessary.

The examiner's car should move more slowly so that the subject's car passes the examiner's and so that the examiner's car is *not* at the end of the road when the subject says, "Stop."

Note that the subject's car has traveled faster and further than the examiner's automobile.

Requestioning:

Ask:	Correct Response
DID THE CARS START MOVING AT THE SAME TIME?	Yes
DID THE CARS STOP MOVING AT THE SAME TIME?	Yes
DID ONE CAR MOVE FURTHER THAN THE OTHER CAR?	Yes

DID ONE CAR MOVE FOR
A LONGER TIME THAN THE OTHER?　　　No

If the child answers, "Yes" to the last question then ask,
WHICH CAR?

Requestioning:
　　WHY DO YOU SAY THAT ＿＿＿＿＿＿CAR TRAVELED
FOR A LONGER TIME THAN THE OTHER? If nec-
essary, probe further.

Appraisal:
　UC　Subject understood concept of time & space —
　　　　answered each question correctly.
　　T　Subject partially understood concept of time & space
　　　　— answered at least two questions correctly.
　NH　Subject does not understand concept of time and
　　　　space — answered three or more questions *incorrectly*.

Comment:
　The child's mode of thinking often differs and he may
maintain that since his automobile traveled a greater
distance, the examiner's auto must have started later or
stopped sooner.

TASK 22: CONCEPT OF AGE

Materials:

Set of pictures showing growth of trees. Six apple trees and five pear trees. (See Appendix B.) A set of dogs is also available for this task in Appendix B.

Situation:

Show the subject the six pictures of the apple tree. Say, HERE ARE PICTURES OF AN APPLE TREE I PLANTED IN MY YARD. PLACE THE PICTURES IN ORDER TO SHOW ME HOW THE TREE GREW. PUT THE DRAWING OF THE YOUNGEST TREE HERE AND THE OLDEST TREE HERE. (Use left to right progression.) SHOW ME HOW THE TREE GREW.

Be sure the child is able to seriate the trees. If he has trouble, be sure the trees are in the proper growth order and he understands if they must be changed. If difficulty arises in arranging the trees in their proper order, this task will be unsuccessful since the child possesses inadequate knowledge for seriation.

Say, ONE YEAR AFTER I PLANTED THE APPLE TREE, I PLANTED A PEAR TREE IN MY YARD. HERE ARE DRAWINGS OF THE PEAR TREE. (Show subject the smallest tree.) Say, THIS IS A DRAWING OF THE PEAR TREE WHEN I FIRST PLANTED IT. The examiner should place the drawing of the smallest pear tree above the second apple tree and say, PUT THESE DRAWINGS IN ORDER TO SHOW ME HOW THE PEAR TREE GREW. Ask, LOOK AT ALL THE TREES AND TELL ME WHICH ONE IS THE OLDEST TREE THIS YEAR.

Requestioning:

HOW DO YOU KNOW THE _____TREE IS THE OLDEST? ARE YOU CERTAIN THAT THE _____TREE IS THE OLDEST?

110

Appraisal:

UC   Subject recognized the apple tree was older.

 T   Subject vacillated answer upon requestioning.

NH   Subject believed the pear tree was older.

Comment:

To young children aging is a continuous process related to size. For many young children when a person stops growing, he also stops getting older. If a person is taller than another, he is automatically older. (Try this experiment in your school. Show the child a tall teacher who is younger than a short teacher. If the child has problems with this concept, he will believe that the tall teacher is automatically the older of the two.) A child does not necessarily associate age differences between people with the order of their birth. In order to heighten interest, the examiner may wish to use the dogs which appear in Appendix B.

TASK 23: TIME MEASUREMENT I

Materials:
One minute egg timer. See comment below.
Stop watch or large watch with a second hand.
Blocks or Cuisenaire rods in large container and one empty container.

Situation:
Show the subject the one minute egg timer and demonstrate what happens to the sand. Say, PUT THE OBJECTS THAT ARE IN THIS CONTAINER INTO THE OTHER CONTAINER AS FAST AS YOU CAN! WHEN ALL THE SAND HAS GONE TO THE BOTTOM OF THE GLASS, I WILL TELL YOU TO STOP. When the timer's sand is in the bottom, direct the subject to stop. Then tell the child, NOW PLACE THE OBJECTS *VERY SLOWLY AND CAREFULLY* BACK INTO THE ORIGINAL CONTAINER.

Ask, DID THE SAND RUN AS FAST WHEN YOU WERE PUTTING THE OBJECTS IN THIS CONTAINER (the empty one) OR DID THE SAND RUN FASTER THE OTHER TIME?

Requestioning:
ARE YOU SURE THE SAND MOVED FASTER? OR SLOWER? OR THE SAME? HOW DO YOU KNOW THIS?

Appraisal:
- UC Subject answered that speed of the sand was constant, understood the concept of velocity.
- T Subject not certain and/or did not understand the problem.
- NH Subject answered that the speed of the sand changed.

Comment:

Time is measured in conventional ways which utilize the movement of objects such as the second hand of a watch, an egg timer, etc. This concept seems so elementary that we sometimes forget that children believe the speed of sand or the second hand of a clock is influenced by the rate of their own motion. The child approaches this in an egocentric fashion — if he moves fast; then so does time. Likewise, if he is engaged in an unenjoyable task; time "drags." (This concept often seems to apply to adults — when performing an enjoyable task, time "flies.") These tasks help the early childhood teacher to understand the nature of these misconceptions. [Note: some teachers have experienced difficulty obtaining a one minute egg timer. These can often be found in a gourmet or specialty shop. If not available you can convert a three minute timer as follows: Obtain a high speed electric drill like a Dremel Moto Tool or a Craftsman Hobby Tool and attach a small emery wheel. Using the emery wheel, gently drill a small hole in the top of the "hourglass" near the spot where the tube was formed by the glassblower. When a hole has been made, remove about 2/3 of the sand —leaving approximately 1/3 in the container. Cover the hole with a dab of glue. If an egg timer is not available, you can use a watch or clock with a large second hand.]

TASK 24: TIME MEASUREMENT II

Materials:

Stopwatch with a sweep second hand.
Metronome "set" to beat at one second intervals.
Round piece of paper or cardboard cut to cover the face of the watch.

Situation:

Show the child the metronome and explain the way it works. Suggestion: Allow extra time for experimentation to help the child understand the apparatus and allow time for curiosity. Say, COUNT TO 15 WITH THE BEAT OF THE METRONOME.

Show the child the stopwatch and the second hand. Discuss the relationship between the distance covered by the second hand and the fifteen beats of the metronome. Repeat the counting, if necessary.

Mask the stop watch and ask the child to count to 15 more quickly. (The metronome should continue to beat at the preset speed.) Ask the child to predict how far the hand on the stop watch has traveled during the more rapid count.

Requestioning:

WHY DO YOU SAY THAT? DID THE CLOCK MOVE FASTER WHEN YOU COUNTED FASTER?

Appraisal:

UC   Subject answered that the second hand would be somewhere between 0 and 15.

T   Subject has some knowledge of time. He may indicate that he counted faster than the clock moved — he is unable to translate this observation into a time frame.

NH   Subject answered that placement of the second hand was somewhere beyond 15 or that the clock moved faster or subject was unable to give a meaningful response.

Comment:

See comments in Task 23.

CHAPTER 6

Spatial Relations

In many instances early childhood educators do not fully understand the application of spatial reasoning (topology) for young children. Children who understand the logic of number, the concept of spatial relations, and the concept of temporal relations are normally considered in a "readiness stage" for more formalized instruction. They are capable of thinking in semi-concrete terms and, on occasion, can conceptualize at an abstract level. Piaget has shown that the concept of number, space, and time combine to form a synthesis for the basis of logical thought. Children who have not achieved this level of thought and understanding will experience some degree of confusion, frustration and even failure. Unless they fully understand children's reasoning related to spatial relations, teachers may include concepts in the curriculum which are inappropriate.

Let us examine the development of spatial relations. The newborn does not possess spatial awareness in any true sense of the word. The neonate originally perceives only the self and this self comprises all awareness. As Piaget (1969, p. 13) has stated, " . . . the child's initial universe is entirely centered on his own body . . . " Through the sucking reflex, via use of the mouth and visual observation, the child begins to recognize other objects occupying other spaces. Thus, the child begins the initial separation of self and "nonself" (mother, bed, bottle, rug, floor) and learns he is a single object moving among other objects along some life space continuum. Research data do not show when or how this knowledge of self and nonself occurs. Since it is three to four months before the child can sit up or crawl; about a year before he can walk — his knowledge of space is necessarily limited to objects which someone gives him or materials which come into his immediate purview.

115

Thus, it would appear that the child's spatial knowledge is initially acquired through objects brought to him or objects which he can view from his crib or wherever else the adult places him. The *proximity* of objects controls his spatial awareness. As his awareness expands he begins to separate objects from himself and to separate objects from each other. He relates to objects in terms of his own body. For example: "The things I can reach and the things I cannot reach." As the child begins to differentiate where one object ends and another begins, *perceptual separation* emerges. After the child learns to separate objects in his spatial field, he learns the mastery of *ordering*.

At four or five months if a child is presented with a baby bottle with the blunt end first, he will not know what to do with the bottle. By the eighth month, however, the child recognizes that a bottle has a reverse side and turns the bottle to the nipple end (*constancy of object*). During this period the child begins to recognize that an object exists even when it is out of view. The infant will now begin to search for a hidden object (*object permanence*). As his awareness expands, the child sees that certain objects may be arranged in relation to each other (*order*).

Ultimately the child learns *enclosure* — that some items are enclosed by or surrounded by other objects. Thus, he can finally perceive and react to the totality of his spatial field; his crib, playroom, family room, house.

The concept of *continuity* is learned when the child understands that a spatial field is continuous. A spatial field can be his mother's face or the view from a tree house. When the child is able to coordinate the first four levels of topological reasoning — proximity, separation, order, and enclosure, he normally comprehends spatial continuity. The child who reaches for his juice and ends up with the bowl of jello has not achieved spatial continuity. He is unable to expand his spatial field from the bowl of jello to include part of his high chair tray.

Spatial reasoning is related to many of the cognitive tasks mentioned in this book. The child having difficulty seriating sticks for apple trees is also having difficulty with spatial order. The child unable to conserve number when chips are spread out is obviously confusing number with spatial proximity. The youngster who can make graphic classifications is utilizing the concept of proximity.

In the preoperational stage, the child is still perception bound and cannot imagine how an object will look except as he views it from his particular vantage point. In discussing space, Piaget has postulated that children grasp topological ideas first; that is, spatial relations and forms without shape. By three to four years of age children can distinguish open and closed figures. However, most children are five years of age before they can copy a square — at least sufficiently to show a knowledge of angles. Duplicating squares and other polygons indicates the beginning of geometric awareness.

Spatial awareness also deals with *projective* ability. The word, projective, refers to spatial perception of one's "point of view" and is related to spatial reasoning. An example of the use of projective ability in space is an artistic rendition of a forest with a flowing stream. In actuality the stream may be several feet wide but appears narrow at one point to give the appearance of distance. Drawing trees and other objects in perspective can give the appearance of height and depth.

In one experiment Piaget placed two small posts (A and B) fifteen inches apart and asked children to place five other posts in a straight line between A and B. The preschool child placed the posts in terms of the immediately preceeding one rather than in reference to the imaginary line between A and B. By the age of seven, most children could construct a straight row of posts between A and B. Before the age of seven the child uses his knowledge of proximity, separation, and order to build his line but will not use any projective skills. He will not consider checking the straightness of the line by closing one eye or by sighting. The child who uses a straight edge to calculate demonstrates an initial understanding of the concept of measurement.

In another experiment the child is shown a doll viewing a pencil. The child is then shown a series of pictures of the pencil and asked to select the picture depicting the doll's point of view. Usually children cannot successfully perform this task until they are seven to eight years of age.

During the preoperational stage the child develops many concepts which aid in spatial reasoning. The most important development relates to the child's ability to represent spatial concepts and mental images. Appropriate experiences for the preschool child utilizing spatial concepts are varied. Representation of space might include identifying shapes by touch rather than sight, predicting the shape of paper before it is folded, describing an object as if the child was viewing it from the other side, utilizing movement and creative dance, or observing the pendulum movement of a swing, or teeter-totter.

An important aspect of spatial reasoning is related to visual perception. The child's early art work, his scribblings and figures, provide insight into his understanding of the spatial world. Usually the earliest drawings of a human are made during the preoperational period. These drawings may be revealing in terms of the child's view of self. Although he may know he has hands and feet, his initial drawings usually consist of a large circle with two to four lines emerging from the circle. When the child begins to add body parts (eyes, hands, mouth, nose, waist, etc.) he is broadening his concept of body image via visual representation. The teacher should record these representational changes in the child's schema.

As he draws self-portraits, the child generally draws other objects on the paper revolving around himself. This is typical of his thinking since he is highly egocentric. As spatial relations develop, the child begins to draw base lines on his paper and all objects tend to be positioned on the base line. He notices that he stands on the floor, the chairs are on the floor, and the table is on the floor. The child's drawings begin to show this type of conceptualization in the latter part of the preoperational stage. Kellogg (1970) and Goodrow (1977) provide excellent discussions of children's art and stages which occur related to children's drawings.

118

Self-portraits by a group of four year old children

The last type of spatial reasoning discussed deals with *measurement of space.* This concept may be superficially dealt with on the primary level. However, it is not until high school geometry that one is fully exposed to spatial reasoning. The concept of formal measurement is generally introduced in primary grades but it is much later before these concepts can be applied. *One must remember that space is abstract in most respects and actually cannot be seen unless it is enclosed.*

A fundamental concept in measurement of space is the concept of a "plane of reference." Pictures are hung using a place of reference such as the floor, ceiling or a plumb line. Children are constantly exposed to the natural plane of reference of the earth. Children exhibit this awareness in their drawings which reveal base lines for the ground and sky lines for ceilings. A common horizontal reference is the surface of liquid seen in lakes, bathtubs, glasses, and bowls.

A simple experiment involving a bottle of colored water may be used in order to assess the child's ability to use a horizontal plane of reference. (Refer to Task 29.) For example, prior to the age of five, most children are unable to draw the water as a plane surface. Generally preschool youngsters do not grasp this concept and will draw the water as a round blot or a little ball in the bottle. In the next stage of development the child recognizes the horizontal plane but does not generally grasp the concept of a horizontal axis as a frame of reference. When a bottle is tilted, the child's drawing will generally show an increase in the volume but little or no effort will be made to change the surface level of the water. He is not able to show that the bottle of colored water has simply changed position. The child usually represents the water level as parallel to the bottom of the bottle instead of representing the level of water on a parallel plane with the ground or table. Prior to the child's ability to represent the water level on a horizontal axis (tilted bottle) the child usually goes through a transitional stage where he is unable to represent the water surface as level. However, he will show that it is no longer parallel to the base. Instead of using the bottle as a reference point, the child begins to use the table as a parallel reference point — and the water level begins to tilt in the child's drawing but is still inaccurate. By the age of seven or eight children are usually able to represent water levels correctly, using a horizontal plane of reference.

Educational Implications for Spatial Relations.

The teacher must understand the relationship between the child's perception of space and his ability to represent it mentally. Piaget found that a young child cannot visualize the outcome of the most simple type of action until he has seen it performed or has been actively involved in the performance. Until the child has cut through a cylinder or seen hot dogs sliced, he cannot visualize the cross section of the cylinder as a circle. Logical thought in spatial representation is based on perception, which is reinforced by visual and tactile concrete experiences.

Most adults have not actually achieved full conceptual development of spatial reasoning. Many adults cannot tell which direction is north, south, east or west. The lost motorist is often given directions only after the adult has spatially oriented himself by facing in a familiar direction. Some adults draw beautifully in perspective while others have difficulty giving reality to any illustration. Persons having difficulty in geometry often do not conceptualize topological relations. Architects report that clients usually have great difficulty conceptualizing three dimensions from a two-dimensional blueprint. The draftsman, carpenter, engineer, carpet layer, seamstress, airline pilot, artist, and architect rely on their spatial awareness for a career.

Children should be given opportunities to place items near each other (*proximity*), to seriate (*order*), and to empty and fill objects (*enclosure*). The school program provides a number of learning situations which will enhance the mastery of spatial awareness. These include: the block corner, sand box and water play area. In addition, the teacher may display materials which children can view from different vantage points. In the case of older children, the teacher should provide objects which can be drawn from different angles and from varying perspectives. Cloth, paper, and cardboard provide opportunities for cutting and folding. Children can predict patterns and shapes which are made by these manipulations. Practice in sectioning can be accomplished through the use of clay and play dough. Of course, one of the best ways that spatial awareness can be taught is through creative movement. As youngsters learn to dance, skip, jump, and leap, they learn how to traverse through space.

In terms of spatial awareness, children are ready to begin instruction in a reading program when they can meet the following criteria: understand concepts related to body image, develop handedness preference, capable of graphically representing objects in space through drawings, reconstructing and identifying shapes, and sequentially ordering concepts and objects. If a child does not have base lines in his drawings it is probably unfair to ask him to place meaningless balls and sticks on lined paper to create letters. For example, it is frustrating to conform to the lines on paper to make the letter "d" if the child does not feel a need for the line or does not possess the muscular control to hold the pencil properly. The child will attach little meaning to a letter at this time if the other characteristics of readiness have not been exhibited. Once the child exhibits a base line in drawings, understands sequence, and has developed handedness it is the optimal time to begin simple word and letter study. A youngster's ability to conceptualize spatially is related to his background experiences. Discriminating between "d" and "b" or "p" and "q", is a learned phenomenon. The same is true for drawing in perspective.

Once children can sequence and recognize differences in letter forms and name configurations, once they can copy figures and make enclosures of figures — such as squares and circles; they can more easily place letters in the correct order to write their name. The ability to write one's own name is the beginning of decoding skills for reading other children's names, signs and eventually books. The child with initial difficulty in reading is often the child who is not spatially aware of his environment. The child with visual and auditory sequential memory has also developed spatial awareness of his field and exhibits readiness for further reading instruction. The early childhood educator should provide a foundation rich in concrete and motoric experiences to enhance later concepts in spatial relations.

TASK 25: PROJECTION OF A STRAIGHT LINE

Materials:
1 Rectangle piece of construction paper (8½″ x 11″).
2 One inch wooden cubes.
8 Wooden sticks or matches, each set upright in small pieces of clay.

Situation A:
Place the blocks on the paper in front of the subject. Refer to illustration below:

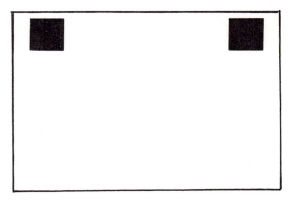

Say, HERE ARE TWO HOUSES AND HERE ARE SOME FENCE POSTS. TAKE THE FENCE POSTS AND MAKE A FENCE FROM THIS HOUSE TO THAT HOUSE. TRY TO MAKE THE FENCE POSTS AS STRAIGHT AS YOU CAN. The examiner should not trace the straight line with the finger, but be sure that the child understands the instructions. Allow the child to work without any aid and do not stop him if he makes a mistake. The process he uses will often be more meaningful than the outcome.

Appraisal: (Part a)

UC   Subject constructed line using metric technique. (Used some type straight edge — like his arm — to line up sticks.)

T   Subject constructed line using projective techniques. (Some type sighting system used to make the line.) Example: Subject used line of sight by looking over the two end sticks.

NH   Subject constructed line using topological concepts. (Proximity, order — achieved a crooked or wavy line.)

Comment:

Refer to the discussion in this chapter. The examiner should draw a representation of the final product on the protocol.

Situation B:

The entire process is repeated with the blocks placed in diagonal corners of the construction paper. Refer to illustration below:

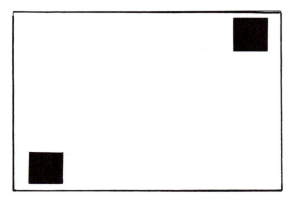

Appraisal: (Part b)

UC Subject constructed line using some metric technique.

T Subject constructed line using projective technique.

NH Subject constructed line using only topological concepts.

Comment:

Examiner should draw a representation of the final product on the protocol. The second situation is more difficult than the first since the child no longer has the straight edge of the the paper or the table to use as a point of reference for aligning the fence posts.

TASK 26: LOCATION OF POSITIONS I

Materials:

2 sheets of 8½″ x 11″ paper for landscapes (See Appendix B.)
Two sets of the following items:
  1 red one inch cube
  1 yellow Cuisenaire rod
  3 white Cuisenaire rods
  2 small plastic men (soldier, cowboy, etc.)

Situation:

The subject should be seated across the table from the examiner. Place the two landscapes on the table in front of the child and arrange them so they are facing in the same direction. Say, HERE ARE TWO DRAWINGS THAT ARE JUST ALIKE. BOTH HAVE A ROAD FOR CARS AND RAILROAD TRACKS FOR TRAINS. (Point to the road and the tracks as the drawings are described.)

Say, NOW I WILL TAKE THIS DRAWING AND YOU MAY USE THE OTHER ONE. (Point to the appropriate landscape.) NOW WE WILL PLACE BUILDINGS ON OUR PICTURES SO THAT BOTH PICTURES WILL LOOK JUST THE SAME. SEE, I AM PLACING A RED BUILDING RIGHT HERE. (See example on the protocol or in Appendix B.) NOW YOU PLACE A RED BUILDING ON YOUR DRAWING. BE SURE YOUR BUILDING IS IN THE SAME PLACE SO THAT OUR PICTURES ARE JUST ALIKE. After the subject has placed the red block the examiner continues, NOW WE ARE GOING TO PUT A YELLOW BUILDING HERE. The examiner continues in this manner and finally places the white buildings as illustrated on the protocol or in the appendix.

Appraisal:

  UC   Subject reproduced picture exactly — all five blocks.

    T   Subject reproduced part of the picture — 3 or 4 blocks.

  NH   Subject was unable to reproduce the picture — 0-2 blocks.

Comment:

As the child places each block, the examiner records the subject's placement on the protocol by: a) placing a checkmark inside each figure the child placed correctly, or b) making a drawing on the landscape where the child made the incorrect placement.

TASK 27: LOCATION OF POSITIONS II

Note: If the subject was unsuccessful in Task 26, it is not necessary to administer Task 27. If placement of the blocks was relatively accurate, then Task 27 may be given.

Materials:
Same as Task 26

Situation:
Turn the examiner's landscape 180° and explain, NOW I AM TURNING MY PICTURE SO THAT I CAN SEE IT BETTER. IT IS STILL JUST LIKE YOURS, BUT TURNED AROUND. Point to each object so subject can determine that it is just the same but turned around. Say, HERE IS A MAN (COWBOY, SOLDIER) FOR YOU AND ONE FOR ME. I AM PLACING MY MAN IN MY PICTURE AND YOU PLACE YOUR MAN IN YOUR PICTURE IN THE SAME PLACE THAT MY MAN IS PLACED.

The examiner places the man on the landscape first in position "A" on the drawing and then records where the child places his man. (Refer to the illustration on the protocol or in Appendix B.)

The examiner then moves her man to position "B" and directs the child to do the same. Then, in order the examiner moves the man to positions, "C", "D", "E", and "F".

Appraisal:
UC   Subject placed man correctly in all six positions.

T   Subject placed man correctly in three to five positions.

NH   Subject failed to place man correctly — 0-2 positions.

Comment:

The examiner should record each position the subject designates. Recording should be made as follows: a) If correct, check or circle the letter shown on the protocol. b) If incorrect, show the position of by writing the letter at the appropriate position on the protocol.

TASK 28: SPATIAL REPRESENTATION OF SELF

Materials:
Four drawings of a face or head (See Appendix B).

Situation A:
Display picture of the back of head view. Say, SHOW ME HOW YOU WOULD STAND FOR ME TO SEE YOU LIKE THIS DRAWING.

Situation B:
Display picture of right profile. Say, SHOW ME HOW YOU WOULD STAND FOR ME TO SEE YOU LIKE THIS DRAWING.

Situation C:
Display picture of left profile. Say, SHOW ME HOW YOU WOULD STAND FOR ME TO SEE YOU LIKE THIS DRAWING.

Situation D:
Display picture of full face view. Say, SHOW ME HOW YOU WOULD STAND FOR ME TO SEE YOU LIKE THIS DRAWING.

Appraisal:
UC   Score UC for each situation where the subject assumed the correct position. Score NH for each incorrect response. (There is no transition category for Task 28.)

    a. Back to examiner.
    b. Facing examiner's right.
    c. Facing examiner's left.
    d. Facing examiner.

Comment:

This task requires that the child physically portray the view of another individual. While the task seems quite simple for most adults, it is difficult for many children. If the child assumes an incorrect position the behavior and the position should be recorded on the protocol. It should be noted that the child who cannot perform on this task will also have difficulty performing on tasks requiring lateral knowledge. An example of an activity requiring lateral knowledge is the "Hokey Pokey." Activities of this type give children experience in "mirroring" and the teacher should include several activities of this type in her program. Note: There are some situations where adults may experience difficulty in performing tasks which require lateral knowledge. On occasion one can observe a person "touching" their wedding band to confirm "left" or "right."

TASK 29: SPATIAL REPRESENTATION OF WATER LEVEL

Materials:

One ten ounce bottle partially filled with red water.
One red crayon.
Pictures showing a bottle in positions as shown in Appendix B.

Situation:

Display the bottle partially filled with water and call attention to the water level. The subject should be at eye level with the bottle so that he can see the edge of the surface.

A. Give the subject picture A. Say, DRAW A PICTURE OF THE WATER JUST AS IT IS IN THE BOTTLE. (Give the child a copy of picture A and allow him to draw the waterline on the picture.)

B. Give the subject picture B and say, PRETEND THAT THE BOTTLE IS TILTED — LIKE IT IS IN THIS PICTURE. DRAW THE WAY THE WATER WILL LOOK WHEN IT IS TILTED. (Give the child a copy of picture B and allow him to draw the waterline on the picture.)

C. Give the subject picture C and say, PRETEND THE BOTTLE IS LYING ON ITS SIDE . . . DRAW THE WAY THE WATER WILL LOOK. (Repeat the procedure performed in #1 and #2.)

D. Cover the pictures shown and tilt the bottle of water and ask the subject to draw a picture of the water just as it is in the bottle. (Note: Position D in Appendix B shows the way the bottle should be tilted.)

E. Place the bottle on its side and repeat the procedure. (Note: Position E in Appendix B shows the position of the bottle.)

F. Ask the subject to color the water as it would be if the bottle were capped and turned upside down. (See Appendix B — picture F.)

Appraisal:

UC Subject correctly projected water levels. Understands spatial representation of water levels.

T Subject correctly drew water level only when viewing the actual water level in bottle.

NH Subject incorrectly projected water level by prediction and actual viewing of water level in the bottle. Does not understand spatial representation of water level.

Comment:

Refer to the discusion earlier in this chapter. Reproduce the child's drawing of the water levels on the protocol. It is not unusual for a child to incorrectly draw the water level even after viewing the water level in the bottle when it is tilted or in a side view.

CHAPTER SEVEN

Reasoning Skills

One of the most fascinating things about teaching young children is the opportunity to look into their world and examine their method of perceiving things. At the end of this chapter some tasks and observations are suggested which provide the teacher with insight into the way children reason and develop their reasoning ability. In the early years of his research (1925-1930), Piaget examined the way in which children explain certain phenomena and provided reasons for their behavior. As children grow and develop between the sensori-motor period and the level of formal operations, the manner and method by which they reason changes dramatically.

In the sensori-motor period we do not see examples of reasoning ability except as children appear to engage in simple functional reasoning. For example, "If you shake a rattle, it makes noise." Between the ages of two to five the preoperational child displays two types of reasoning. Initially reasoning occurs in simple concrete situations which are based upon previous knowledge. We see this type of reasoning when the nursery school child observes the teacher getting napkins and crackers and announces, "Miss Susan is getting juice!" During this period children may make inaccurate judgements because their reasoning is often based on outward appearances. For example, in the DeVries study mentioned in Chapter One, the child "reasoned" that a cat had become "transformed" into a dog because its face had taken on the appearance of a dog.

Piaget also cites a second type of reasoning which he termed, *transductive*. Transductive may be defined as reasoning from one particular to another particular. In transductive reasoning the child sees a relationship between two concrete objects or events where one does not actually exist. For example, one Sunday afternoon we decided to go to a nearby park for a "quickie" picnic with our three-year-old daughter. We hastily prepared a few sandwiches, some potato chips, three canned drinks, napkins and paper plates. These items were placed in a large paper bag. On the way to the park, our daughter started crying and said, "We can't have a picnic because we forgot to bring a picnic basket!" In spite of our assurances to the contrary, we had to return home to get a picnic basket.

In the preoperational and concrete operational period young children become highly confused by complex metaphors, proverbs or even by ordinary day-to-day events. In one experiment Piaget related a series of proverbs to a group of eight to ten year old children and asked them to explain each statement. Proverbs like, "When the cat is away, the mice will play," were often confusing to children and they were unable to correctly assess the meaning of the statement.

Piaget reported that children often arrive at faulty conclusions through two types of reasoning. These types are: *syncretic* and *juxtaposition*. In syncretic thought the child attempts to present a logical explanation regardless of the circumstance. Ginsburg and Opper (1969, 110), state: "Syncretism is a tendency to connect a series of separate ideas into one confused whole . . . In a sense, syncretism is a case of assimilation gone wild. The child does not accommodate to the real meaning of the statement, rather he assimilates it into his own scheme." In syncretic thought the youngster attempts to reconcile or combine opposing principles. For example, "Fish live in the water. They swim because God took away their legs. Goldfish swim faster than guppies because they are yellow."

In juxtaposition, one event is superimposed on another without apparent logical reason. For example, "I ate dinner because I am not hungry!" or "Water gets hot because the fire turned it on." In juxtaposition the child recognizes that certain events are related but fails to logically establish cause and effect.

In a television study several years ago the authors queried a group of 8- to 11-year-old boys about the TV series, *"Hogan's Heroes."* The following comments illustrate the

135

confusion the youngsters had concerning events which occurred in the series. (E represents questions from the examiner. A represents a reply from one of the boys.)

E: Is *Hogan's Heroes* true?

A: Yes, it is real.

E: Is the United States at war with Germany now?

A: Yes.

E: Are the guys on TV really in a prison camp?

A: Yes, the TV cameras are there so we will know what a prison camp is like.

E: Is Hogan really an American soldier?

A: Yes, Hogan is a real colonel.

E: Is Schultz real?

A: Yes, he is really a German guard.

E: Are all the guys soldiers?

A: No, Richard Dawson isn't really a soldier.

E: How do you know?

A: Because he is on *Family Feud* right after *Hogan's Heroes*. They let Richard Dawson out of the prison camp to do the *Family Feud* show.

E: And then what happens?

A: Well, Richard Dawson is really an actor but he has to go back to the prison camp every night.

It is obvious that the boys were confused about the television show in several respects. They incorrectly reason that: a) The United States was at war with Germany; b) the actors were actually soldiers; and c) Richard Dawson was actually in prison camp. The incongruities in their reasoning do not appear to bother them. In this instance the boys take the information and "make it fit" into their perception of the reality.

In formal operations the teenager is capable of a more advanced form of logic. While the preoperational child uses transductive reasoning, the adolescent can utilize the process of *deduction* — that is, reasoning from the general to the particular. (For example: If "all dogs have fleas" and we see a particular dog, we may deduce that he, too, has fleas.) In addition, mature individuals are also capable of *inductive* thought — that is, reasoning from the particular to the general. Thus, if we encounter a large group of kindergarten teachers who are patient and nurturant, we might reasonably conclude that kindergarten teachers possess the traits of patience and nurturance.

The mature person can utilize what has been termed "the scientific method." This view incorporates a systematic approach to problem solving — that is, generating hypotheses, testing them, making predictions and drawing conclusions. In addition, the individual is capable of recursive thought. In recursive thinking, a person has the ability to "think about thinking." The individual is capable of thinking about abstract concepts and of objectively viewing a problem from several vantage points in an objective manner. Often, to the chagrin of his parents, the teenager can evaluate the strengths and weaknesses of an argument with the same facility as grown-ups. The youngster can effectively challenge the logic of an argument and is capable of showing others (particularly his parents) the fallacies in an argument.

In formal operations the person can test the logical truth of Aristotelian-type propositions. In contrast, the concrete operational child can only analyze the logic of a single proposition. Task G, presented at the end of this chapter, illustrates the difference in approach between these two levels of reasoning. For example, let us consider the following syllogism:

Major proposition: All dogs are animals.
Minor proposition: All animals are red.
Conclusion: All dogs are red.

The child in the level of concrete operations will judge each proposition separately. In doing so, he will recognize the absurdity of the minor proposition and determine that the conclusion is also incorrect. Thus, the child will make a judgement based on his actual knowledge and experience. On the other hand, the child who is operating at the level of formal operations will *syllogize logically.* Thus, he will reason: *If* all dogs are animals, and *if* all animals are red —then it follows *logically,* even if not *realistically,* that "all dogs are red." Most teens enjoy this newly acquired skill of being able to think symbolically and "playing with thinking."

Scoring for the Reasoning Skills Tasks.

Chapter Seven contains the first seven tasks in Set II and these are *lettered* A to G. These tasks are designed primarily for youngsters in the concrete operational stage or in the early stages of formal operations — seven to fourteen years. Scoring for the tasks in Set II is slightly different from the tasks in Set I. Tasks A to E contain problems which yield a specific answer. The teacher should record these tasks as follows: A correct response is scored as UC — understands the concept. An incorrect response is scored NH — needs help. Task F (the proverbs) and Task G (the syllogism) are also scored UC and NH. UC would indicate that the child understood the proverbs and the syllogism.

TASK A: CONVERSIONS
"The best buy!"

Materials:
Pencil & paper.
Problems 1, 2, & 3 — below.

Situation:
Say, I AM GOING TO GIVE YOU SOME PROBLEMS
TO SOLVE. IF YOU WISH, YOU MAY USE A PENCIL
AND PAPER TO MAKE THESE COMPUTATIONS.
(Give the child pencil and paper.) Present each problem 1, 2,
and 3. Allow the child sufficient time to solve each problem.

1. You are at a grocery store and wish to buy some rice.
However, you have only a limited amount of money so you
wish to get the "best buy" possible. Assume that the brands
of rice are equal in quality. You look at three boxes of rice:
One contains 14 oz. and sells for 49 cents. One contains 14
oz. and sells for 53 cents. One contains 28 oz. and sells for 93
cents. Which is the best buy? How did you come to that
conclusion?

2. While you are at the grocery store you also wish to
purchase some laundry detergent and want to get the "best
buy." Would you buy 20 oz. of Tide for 95 cents or 49 oz. of
Fab for $2.05? Why? How did you arrive at your answer?

3. While you are in the store you make one final purchase.
You decide to purchase some peanut butter. Which is the
best buy? 12 oz. of Superman Peanut Butter for $1.29; 18 oz.
for $1.71; 28 oz. for $2.89. How did you arrive at your
answer?

Requestioning:
Probe to see how the child perceives of the problem. Say,
HOW DO YOU THINK YOU CAN SOLVE THIS PROB-
LEM? or HOW DID YOU ARRIVE AT THE ANSWER?

Appraisal:

UC   Subject solved problem.

NH   Subject was unable to solve problem.

Comment:

These tasks are primarily for children who are in the final stages of concrete operations or in the early stages of formal operations. If the subject is unable to solve problems 1 and 2, you may omit 3 — since it is the most difficult. This task yields a specific answer. There is no T category, "in transition," for the tasks lettered A to G. Some youngsters will be unable to solve these problems because they cannot use abstract reasoning. Some children will not have mastered the particular math skill. Probe to determine how they approach the problem.

TASK B: CONVERSIONS
Fractions

Materials:
Pencil & paper.
Problems 1, 2, & 3 — below.

Situation:
Say, I AM GOING TO GIVE YOU SOME PROBLEMS TO SOLVE. IF YOU WISH, YOU MAY USE A PENCIL AND PAPER TO MAKE THESE COMPUTATIONS. (Give the child pencil and paper.) Present each problem 1, 2, and 3. Allow the child sufficient time to solve each problem.

1. Here are two fractions. Which is the largest? 3/4 or 3/8?
2. Here are four fractions. Which one is the closest to 5/8?
   1/4   1/2   7/8   8/5
3. This problem is a little more difficult. Here are four fractions. Which one is the closest to 3/16?
   1/8   1/4   3/8   5/32

Requestioning;
Probe to see how the child perceives of the problem. Say, HOW DO YOU THINK YOU CAN SOLVE THIS PROBLEM? or HOW DID YOU ARRIVE AT THE ANSWER?

Appraisal:
UC   Subject solved problem.
NH   Subject was unable to solve problem.

Comment:
These tasks are primarily for children who are in the final stages of concrete operations or in the early stages of formal operations. If the subject is unable to solve problems 1 and 2, you may omit 3 — since it is the most difficult. This task yields a specific answer. There is no T category, "in transition," for the tasks lettered A to G.

TASK C: CONVERSIONS
Time & Distance.

Materials:
Pencil & paper.
Problems 1, 2, & 3 — below.

Situation:
Say, I AM GOING TO GIVE YOU SOME PROBLEMS TO SOLVE. IF YOU WISH, YOU MAY USE A PENCIL AND PAPER TO MAKE THESE COMPUTATIONS. (Give the child pencil and paper.) Present each problem 1, 2, and 3. Allow the child sufficient time to solve each problem

1. You are going on a trip. You are going 50 miles an hour. How far will you go in 2½ hours?

2. You are going on another trip. You will still average 50 miles an hour. The trip is 175 miles long. How long will it take you to make this trip?

3. This problem is a little more difficult. You are going on another trip. You leave at 11 o'clock in the morning from Atlanta. You are going to Mobile, Alabama. Atlanta is in the Eastern Time Zone. Mobile is in the Central Time Zone which means that there is a time difference of one hour between Mobile and Atlanta. You will average 40 miles an hour on your trip. On the way you stop in Birmingham for 15 minutes, so add this amount of time in your computations. The distance to Mobile from Atlanta is 260 miles. What time will you arrive in Mobile?

Requestioning:
Probe to see how the child perceives of the problem. Say, HOW DO YOU THINK YOU CAN SOLVE THIS PROBLEM? or HOW DID YOU ARRIVE AT THE ANSWER?

Appraisal:
UC Subject solved problem.
NH Subject was unable to solve problem.

Comment:

These tasks are primarily for children who are in the final stages of concrete operations or in the early stages of formal operations. If the subject is unable to solve problems 1 and 2, you may omit 3 — since it is the most difficult. This task yields a specific answer. There is no T category, "in transition," for the tasks lettered A to G. Some youngsters will be unable to solve these problems because they cannot use abstract reasoning. Some children will not have mastered the particular math skill. Probe to determine how they approach the problem.

TASK D: AGE PROBLEMS

Mateials:
Pencil & paper.
Problems 1, 2, & 3 — below.

Situation:
Say, I AM GOING TO GIVE YOU SOME PROBLEMS
TO SOLVE. IF YOU WISH, YOU MAY USE A PENCIL
AND PAPER TO MAKE THESE COMPUTATIONS.
(Give the child pencil and paper.) Present each problem 1, 2,
and 3. Allow the child sufficient time to solve each problem.

1. Susan is twelve years old. Sally is two years older than
Susan. How old is Sally?

2. Mark is ten years old. He is four years older than Joan.
When Joan is ten years old, how old will Mark be?

3. This one is a little more difficult. Mary is twenty four
years old now. Mary is twice as old as Ann was, when she
was as old as Ann is now. How old is Ann?

Requestioning:
Probe to see how the child perceives of the problem Say,
HOW DO YOU THINK YOU CAN SOLVE THIS PROB-
LEM? or HOW DID YOU ARRIVE AT THE ANSWER?

Appraisal:
UC   Subject solved problem.
NH   Subject was unable to solve problem.

Comment:
These tasks are primarily for children who are in the final
stages of concrete operations or in the early stages of formal
operations. If the subject is unable to solve problems 1 and
2, you may omit 3 — since it is the most difficult. This task
yields a specific answer. There is no T category, "in
transition," for the tasks lettered A to G.

TASK E: PREDICTION PROBLEMS

Materials:
  Pencil and paper.
  Problems 1, 2, & 3 — below.

Situation:
  Say, HERE ARE SOME PROBLEMS. LOOK AT THE ONE I HAVE ON THE PAPER. (Show the subject problem "x". Explain the following procedure.) Say, IN THIS PROBLEM THERE IS A "2" AND A "BLANK" . . . AND AN "=" SIGN AND A "3." IF YOU MAKE THE EQUATION TRUE, YOU SHOULD HAVE TO PLACE A "PLUS" HERE (Show the correct location) AND A "1" IN THE BLANK. (Show correct location.) After you see that the subject understands the sample, let him work the other problems.

  x) 2 _____ $= 3$ $(2 + 1 = 3)$
  1. 3 _____ $= 5$
  2. 6 _____ $+ 2 = 5$
  3. 15 _____ $x\ 3 = 27$

Requestioning:
  Probe to see how the child perceives of the problem. Say, HOW DO YOU THINK YOU CAN SOLVE THIS PROBLEM? or HOW DID YOU ARRIVE AT THE ANSWER?

Appraisal:
  UC   Subject solved problem.
  NH   Subject was unable to solve problem.

Comment:
  These tasks are primarily for children who are in the final stages of concrete operations or in the early stages of formal operations. This task yields a specific answer. There is no T category, "in transition," for the tasks lettered A to G.

TASK F: PROVERBS

Materials:
   Proverbs which are presented below. No other material required.

Situation:
   Say, HERE ARE SOME SENTENCES. THEY ARE CALLED PROVERBS. I AM GOING TO READ THEM TO YOU. I WANT YOU TO TELL ME WHAT THEY MEAN.

1. FIGHT FIRE WITH FIRE.
2. A PENNY SAVED IS A PENNY EARNED.
3. STRIKE WHILE THE IRON IS HOT.
4. THE EARLY BIRD GETS THE WORM.
5. A STITCH IN TIME SAVES NINE.
6. A BIRD IN THE HAND IS WORTH TWO IN THE BUSH.

Appraisal:
   UC   Subject understood proverb.
   NH   Subject did not understand proverb.

Comment:
   Several proverbs are presented. Generally children under six years of age will not understand the proverbs. Read the proverb to the child and record his statement. Probe to see how the child arrives at his reasoning. Use at least *three* of the proverbs listed above. As a general rule of thumb, most children have more difficulty with proverbs 4, 5, and 6. If you have a favorite proverb of your own, you may substitute.

TASK G: SYLLOGISM.

Materials:
The syllogism presented below. No other materials are needed.

Situation:
Say, I AM GOING TO TELL YOU SOMETHING WHICH IS CALLED A SYLLOGISM. THAT IS THE NAME FOR THE SPECIAL KIND OF LOGIC. I WILL TELL YOU TWO SENTENCES. THEN, BASED ON THE LOGIC OF THE SENTENCES, I WILL GIVE YOU A CONCLUSION — YOU MUST TELL ME IF THE SENTENCE IS TRUE. Note: do not elaborate on your statement. If the subject is confused, read the statement again. The purpose of this task is to determine if the subject can reason in terms of this particular form of logic — so the examiner should not elaborate or explain further.

Say, IF ALL DOGS ARE ANIMALS.
AND IF ALL ANIMALS ARE RED.
THEN ALL DOGS ARE RED.

Requestioning:
If the youngster still seems confused, repeat the syllogism. Say, ARE ALL DOGS RED? HOW DO YOU KNOW THAT?

Appraisal:
UC   Subject could reason in terms of the major and minor propositions and stated that, IF all animals were red, THEN all dogs would be red also.

NH   Subject did not understand the syllogism and could not follow the reasoning.

Comment:
The child in the level of concrete operations will judge each proposition separately. In doing so, he will recognize the absurdity of the minor proposition and determine that

the conclusion is also incorrect. Thus, the child will make a judgement based on his actual knowledge and experience. On the other hand, the child who is operating at the level of formal operations will *syllogize logically*. Thus, he will reason: *If* all dogs are animals, and *If* all animals are red —then it follows *logically* even if not *realistically,* that "all dogs are red."

CHAPTER EIGHT

Rules and Moral Development

In his book, *The Moral Judgement of the Child,* Piaget discussed how children make rules, establish ideas about lying and stealing and develop a sense of right and wrong. Piaget developed his theories about moral development by watching children play games. As a part of his research he carefully observed several groups of young boys playing marbles and acquired a thorough knowledge of the rules of the game. Piaget believed rule making and moral development were intrinsically related. He felt that the essential feature of morality was the acceptance of a system of rules. We believe that an examination of these stages of moral development and rule making will be helpful to the teacher.

Like cognitive development, Piaget believes that morality progresses through successive stages. These stages are:

1. **The Premoral stage.** (birth to four years). During this period children play in a rather simple motoric fashion. The child does not appear to be aware of rules and does not feel any commitment or obligation to follow the rules. Generally games are simple, short-lived and have no rules. (Examples of games in this period would include, "Peek-a-boo" and rolling a ball to another person.) Premoral children may experience difficulty in telling or recognizing the truth. The inability to conceptualize at this age often causes children to get their facts mixed up and confused.

2. **Egocentric stage.** (4-7 years). In this stage children believe that rules are sacred. However, in spite of this belief, they do not know how to follow rules, but insist that they do. They may become quite angry if they feel they have been punished unjustly. There is almost no feeling of competitiveness and winning does not seem to be too important. General-

ly, the rules established by a child make little sense. Rather there are rules, "Because I say so!" In addition, the rules may change at the whim of the child. Children dichotomize value judgements in terms of "black and white" or "good and bad." Lying is perhaps too strong a term to use for children in the intuitive period — but they do experience great difficulty in separating reality from fantasy. For example, one child will relate an event ("I had a party!") and all the other children will exclaim, "I had a party too!"

3. **Incipient cooperation stage.** (7-10 years). The child focuses on the consequences of an action rather than the intent of the actor. Games begin to take on a distinct social character. The child makes a sincere attempt to follow the rules. He cooperates with his playmates — that is, they can mutually agree to the rules; but there is a spirit of competition. Children at this stage are more knowledgeable about rules and rule setting. In games youngsters can "choose up sides," decide on which team can "go first," and take turns.

4. **Genuine Cooperation.** (11 years to adult). The eleven year old now considers the "intent" of an action as well as the consequences of that action. When the youngster reaches the stage of genuine cooperation he has developed a sense of mastery in terms of the rules. He agrees with the other players on the rules and tries to win the game within this framework. At this age there is often a legalistic fascination with the rules and rule making. Piaget relates an incident involving a group of eleven and twelve year old boys who were preparing to have a snowball fight. The group divided itself into teams, elected a slate of officers, designated a captain and a series of duties for each player. The group established a complicated set of rules and regulations *plus* a series of punishments for rule infractions. In fact, the boys took so much time establishing the teams and the rules that there was no time left to play the game.

In addition to his observations of youngsters playing marbles and other games, Piaget devised several "moral stories." The following anecdotes are typical of Piaget's stories. Note: These stories are also presented in Task H.

> Jim is in his room. His mother calls him to dinner. He goes into the dining room. . . but

there is a chair just behind the door. In the chair there is a tray which has fifteen cups on it. Jim doesn't realize that the tray of cups is behind the door. When he goes into the dining room, the door knocks against the tray and bang go all fifteen cups — and they all get broken.

Just before dinner, Terry's mother had to go next door to borrow some sugar. While she was gone Terry decided to sneak a cookie out of the cupboard. He climbed up on a chair to reach the cookie jar. But the jar was too high and he couldn't reach it. As he got down from the chair he knocked over a cup. The cup fell on the floor and broke.

Following the presentation of these anecdotes Piaget asked, "Which child is naughtier?" and "Who should be punished more severely?" Children in the concrete operational stage usually felt that Jim was naughtier because he broke more cups. Children in the stage of formal operations said that Terry was naughtier because he was attempting to get a cookie without permission. In this example the concrete operational child focuses on the result (breaking fifteen cups vs. breaking one cup) rather than on the intention of the child. Interestingly, we can often find a parallel with some adults. They fail to distinguish an "accidental hurt" from an "intentional hurt." They measure the wrongdoing in terms of its *cost* rather than judging the motivations of the actor.

Kohlberg (1963), a noted psychologist, has revised and modified Piaget's stages of moral development. We believe that his adaptation of the theory can be quite helpful to the teacher. According to Kohlberg, moral development follows a sequence of stages quite similar to the ones expounded by Piaget. He also states that, in general, moral development is achieved internally as a process of growth. Kohlberg presents a beginning stage (Stage 0) plus three levels of moral development. Each level is divided into two substages. Payne (1983, 1, 2), has presented an excellent summary of Kohlberg's developmental stages.

Stage 0. (Birth to 4 years). At this stage, children do not understand rules or obligations and are only concerned about their own pleasure. Thus, what they feel to be good, is good; bad is what hurts or is painful.

Preconventional levels. (4-9 years). (Stage 1): Obedience and punishment orientation. The child's moral decisions are based simply on the fear of authority and avoiding punishment. (Stage 2): Naively selfish orientation. The child believes and acts according to the premise: "What is right is what works!" Behavior exhibited is that which meets personal needs.

Conventional levels. (9-15 years). (Stage 3): Good boy-nice girl orientation. Good behavior is that which pleases or helps others and is approved by them. One earns approval by being "nice." (Stage 4): The "law and order" orientation. A person does "one's duty," shows respect for authority, follows fixed rules, and tries to maintain the existing social order.

Postconventional levels. (16 years to adult). (Stage 5): Social contract legalistic orientation. An awareness of personal rights as guaranteed by society. A strong sense of duty still prevails, but morality is seen as the responsibility to honor contractual agreements and the rights of others. (Stage 6): The universal ethical principle orientation. Right is defined by the decision of conscience in accord with self-chosen ethical principles.

Kohlberg conducted a longitudinal study concerning his stages of moral development. He related a series of stories, each of which contained a "moral dilemma," and then asked youngsters how they would handle the problem. One classic example of the moral stories is the "Heinz dilemma." (Kohlberg 1969, 379.) It goes as follows:

> In Europe, a woman was near death from a special kind of cancer. There was one drug that the doctors thought might save her. It was a form of radium that a druggist in the same town had recently discovered. The drug was expensive to make, but the druggist was charging ten times what the drug cost him to make. He

paid $200 for the radium and charged $2,000 for a small dose of the drug. The sick woman's husband, Heinz, went to everyone he knew to borrow money, but he could only get together about $1,000, which is half of what it cost. He told the druggist that his wife was dying and asked him to sell it cheaper or let him pay later. But the druggist said, "No, I discovered the drug and I'm going to make money from it." So Heinz got desperate and broke into the man's store to steal the drug for his wife. Should the husband have done that?

Actually Kohlberg was not interested in the child's decision on whether or not Heinz should steal the drug. Rather he was concerned with the reasons children gave for their conclusions. Table 8.1 shows some possible courses of action taken in response to the Heinz dilemma. (Kohlberg 1969, 379-380.)

Kohlberg's stages five and six are, in many ways, quite similar to Erikson's sense of integrity and Ausubel's self-actualized persons. There have been several criticisms of Kohlberg's theory. Some researchers feel that the stages are culture bound, highly ethnocentric and represent an American middle-class liberal orientation. Persons have been particularly critical concerning his treatment of stage six. Several investigators have been unable to find this stage with most subjects. Kohlberg has stated that stage six is primarily a hypothetical construct and tends to be representative of famous persons like Gandhi, Martin Luther King and Albert Schweitzer — and is not actually a verifiable construct.

There are several things the teacher and parent can do which will enhance the growth of moral development. One of the major ways children learn moral principles is through observational learning. By modeling the behavior of parents, the teacher, and other significant persons, the child begins to internalize moral precepts. Research studies show that children can gain an understanding of rules and problems through discussions of moral issues and dilemmas. Teachers can present children with "real life" problem situations and provide opportunities for discussion and role playing. Some studies suggest that children develop in moral reasoning ability through social interaction with others. Research shows that children generally understand moral judgements at their own level plus one stage above. Finally, the teacher should listen to the child's statements and actions since these are reflections of his feelings and provide insight into the youngster's stage of moral growth.

Scoring for the Moral Development Tasks.

Chapter Eight contains four tasks in Set II and these are *lettered* H, I, J, and K. These tasks can be used with children from the age of five or six through adolescence — and even into adulthood. There is no scoring for the tasks presented in Chapter Eight. There is no recording of UC, T, or NH. Rather, the examiner should record the child's responses and the reasoning behind the judgements he makes. These replies should be made in the observation notes. In order to assess the level of moral development, examine the stages presented by Piaget and by Kohlberg.

TABLE 8.1

**COURSE OF ACTION TAKEN IN RESPONSE
TO THE HEINZ DILEMMA**

Stage	*Pro*	*Con*
1. Obedience-Punishment Orientation	Heinz should steal the drug. It isn't bad to take it. He tried to pay for it.	He shouldn't steal the drug. He should buy it. He might be put in jail.
2. Naively selfish Orientation	It is alright to steal because he wants wife to live.	The druggist isn't bad; he just wants to make a profit.
3. Good boy-nice girl Orientation	It is natural for a good husband to want to help his wife. He loves her.	If his wife dies, he cannot be blamed. The druggist is selfish.
4. Law & Order Orientation	It is the man's responsibility to care for his wife. Marriage is a legal contract.	It is natural for the husband to want to save his wife, but it is always wrong to steal.
5. Social contract Orientation	Taking drugs isn't right, but it is justified under these circumstances.	You cannot blame husband, but it does not justify taking law into your own hands.
6. Universal-ethical Orientation	Situation forces husband into an act in which it is morally correct to steal.	You can't blame husband but he cannot be selfish. He must consider all of society. End does not justify the means.

155

TASK H: MORAL STORIES I

Materials:

Stories presented below.

Situation:

Tell the child the following stories about Jim and Terry:

A) Jim is in his room. His mother calls him to dinner. He goes into the dining room . . . but there is a chair just behind the door. In the chair there is a tray which has fifteen cups on it. Jim doesn't realize that the tray of cups is behind the door. When he goes into the dining room, the door knocks against the tray and bang go all fifteen cups —and they all get broken.

B) Just before dinner, Terry's mother had to go next door to borrow some sugar. While she was gone Terry decided to sneak a cookie out of the cupboard. He climbed up on a chair to reach the cookie jar. But the jar was too high and he couldn't reach it. As he got down from the chair he knocked over a cup. The cup fell on the floor and broke.

Ask, WHO WAS NAUGHTIER? JIM OR TERRY? Ask, WHO SHOULD BE PUNISHED MORE? WHY DO YOU SAY THAT?

Comment:

There is no scoring for the tasks presented in Chapter Eight. There is no recording of UC, T, or NH. The examiner should record the child's responses and the reasoning behind the judgements he makes. These replies should be made in the observation notes. In order to assess the level of moral development, examine the stages presented by Piaget and by Kohlberg.

TASK I: MORAL STORIES II

Materials:

Story presented below.

Situation:

Tell the child the story about Heinz.

In Europe, a woman was near death from a special kind of cancer. There was one drug that the doctors thought might save her. It was a form of radium that a druggist in the same town had recently discovered. The drug was expensive to make, but the druggist was charging ten times what the drug cost him to make. He paid $200 for the radium and charged $2,000 for a small dose of the drug. The sick woman's husband, Heinz, went to everyone he knew to borrow money, but he could only get together about $1,000, which is half of what it cost. He told the druggist that his wife was dying and asked him to sell it cheaper or let him pay later. But the druggist said, "No, I discovered the drug and I'm going to make money from it." So Heinz got desperate and broke into the man's store to steal the drug for his wife. Should the husband have done that?

Comment:

There is no scoring for the tasks presented in Chapter Eight. There is no recording of UC, T, or NH. The examiner should not be concerned with the child's decision on whether or not Heinz should steal the drug. The examiner should record the child's responses and the reasoning behind the judgements he makes. These replies should be made in the observation notes. The Heinz dilemma can serve as a good discussion for teenagers and college students. In order to assess the level of moral development, examine the stages presented by Kohlberg.

TASK J: MORAL DILEMMA I

Materials:
Situation presented below.

Situation:
Say, YOU HAVE BEEN LEARNING ABOUT NUM-
BERS. THE TEACHER GIVES YOU A TEST TO SEE
HOW MUCH YOU HAVE LEARNED. BUT, YOUR BEST
FRIEND IS HAVING TROUBLE ON THE TEST. WHAT
WOULD YOU DO?

Requestioning:
If the child says he would help his friend ask, HOW
WOULD YOU DO THIS? Ask, WHAT WOULD YOU DO
IF THE TEACHER SAID THAT SHE WANTS EVERY-
BODY TO DO THEIR OWN WORK?

Comment:
This situation is most appropriately used with children in
the 7-11 year age range. There is no scoring for the tasks
presented in Chapter Eight. There is no recording of UC, T,
or NH. The examiner should record the child's responses
and the reasoning behind the judgements he makes. These
replies should be made in the observation notes. In order to
assess the level of moral development, examine the stages
presented by Piaget and by Kohlberg.

TASK K: MORAL DILEMMA II

Materials:
Situation presented below.

Situation:
Say, YOU ARE TAKING A TEST AND IT IS VERY IMPORTANT TO YOU. YOU OBSERVE A PERSON NEARBY WHO IS CHEATING ON THE TEST. WHAT WOULD YOU DO? WOULD YOU (A) TELL THE TEACHER THAT THE PERSON HAD CHEATED. (B) WRITE A NOTE TO THE TEACHER AND TELL HER THAT THE PERSON CHEATED — BUT NOT SIGN THE NOTE. (C) CONFRONT THE PERSON DIRECTLY AND LET HIM KNOW THAT YOU SAW HIM CHEATING. (D) DO NOTHING.

Requestioning:
Probe to determine why the subject made the particular choice. Ask, WHY DID YOU CHOOSE THAT SOLUTION?

Comment:
This situation is particularly appropriate for children seven years and older. It can serve as a good discussion for teenagers and college students. There is no scoring for the tasks presented in Chapter Eight. There is no recording of UC, T, or NH. The examiner should record the child's responses and the reasoning behind the judgements he makes. These replies should be made in the observation notes. In order to assess the level of moral development, examine the stages presented by Piaget and by Kohlberg.

CHAPTER NINE

Language

Success in school often depends on the ability to understand and use language. Language promotes thought and develops in conjunction with cognitive growth.

According to Nimnicht, McAfee and Meier (1969, p. 41) language is crucial "to the processes of labeling, forming concepts, solving problems, making associations, and retrieving information." These authors also point out that the nursery school and kindergarten pay little attention to oral language training and yet "the elementary school curriculum assumes that the child will arrive in first grade with an adequate command of spoken English."

Piaget found that the first words of the infant (sensorimotor stage) are related to the actions they perform or observe first hand. In Piagetian theory, cognitive development determines the course of language growth. "Language does not constitute the source of logic but is, on the contrary, structured by it." (Piaget, 1926, p. 90).

However, as Pflaum-Conner indicated (1978, p. 7): "Even if language does not contribute to the development of logical behavior, it is recognized as a tool of instruction in cognitive development for children who are in transition to the concrete operational period of development."

In contrast to Piaget's theory concerning the role of language, Vygotsky (1962) felt that dialogue was of major importance in stimulating language and cognition. The Russian psychologist also pointed out the role of modeling in enhancing language development and the demonstration of the structure of language.

Bruner has taken a position between Vygotsky and Piaget. He felt that language occupied a stronger role in provoking thought than designated by Piaget — but not quite the major role as viewed by Vygotsky.

These points of view are presented not as scientific laws, but rather as theories. Cazden (1968, p. 131) stated: "Our understanding of the role of environmental assistance in language development is tentative and incomplete . . . even if we knew what produces healthy language development in a natural environment, the difficulty remains of translating this understanding into educational programs."

The Role of the Teacher

In spite of the limitations mentioned by Cazden, a number of researchers and educators have offered suggestions for the role of the teacher in enriching the language curriculum and structuring the class environment.

Leeper, et al, (1979) have suggested that the teacher take time to listen to the child, to be aware of her tone of voice, manner of speaking and vocabulary. The classroom should be comfortable and one in which the child feels free to converse, use language and enjoy the experience.

Pflaum-Conner (1978) discussed the role of the teacher in emphasizing adult-child and child-child dialogue and providing for natural, informal use of expansion.

Lavatelli (1970) reported that small group sessions maximized two-way conversation between teacher and child. (Vygotsky's importance of the dialogue.) She also felt that language training should be carried on in a warm, friendly, supportive environment with the teacher relying more on modeling than on correcting so that the child's associations with language would be pleasant ones.

Robison and Schwartz (1972) also discussed the importance of a healthy supportive environment and providing children with opportunities to talk with adults and children, as well as learning to listen. In addition, they emphasized giving youngsters many opportunities to be *actively involved* in the manipulation of objects, since children learn language meanings through actions.

161

Nimnicht, McAfee and Meier (1969, pp. 45-49) have offered the teacher several guidelines for modeling and developing concepts. In their suggestions these authors recommend using complete sentences. Example: To the child's query of "What's that?," teachers often reply "a fire hat" — rather than using the complete sentence, "This is a fireman's hat."

They also suggest that the teacher use categorization and classifications, when appropriate. Examples: "That *color* is *blue*." "The *apple* is a *fruit*." Other suggestions are offered in terms of references to size, weight and other dimensions and the importance of using specific words rather than general terms. Example: Instead of "Put them away," the teacher might say, "Place the blocks on the shelf."

The foregoing discussion indicates that a number of writers and researchers appear to follow the theoretical considerations postulated by Vygotsky and Bruner. Since the research data do not indicate otherwise, the authors of this text tend to utilize these two points of view and believe that the teacher can enhance language development through modeling, encouraging meaningful dialogue and providing a school setting which is warm, supportive and encourages verbal interaction. Since language is to some extent maturational, the teacher is cautioned to set realistic goals which match the child's gradual acquisition of language. However the writers tend to agree with Piaget's observation that to enhance language acquisition without the child having the appropriate conceptual framework is futile in terms of the long range goals.

The Development of Language

Since children experience certain stages of language development at approximately the same time (even cross-culturally), there is obviously a maturational base to language development. However, since American children learn English; Puerto Rican children — Spanish; and Russian children — Russian; there is obviously a strong experiential base. Irwin (1960), Weisberg (1963), Cazden (1968), and Lennenberg (1967), have demonstrated that an enriched environment can enhance language development.

TABLE 9. 1

NORMS IN LANGUAGE DEVELOPMENT

AGE	VOCABULARY	SYNTAX	PHONOLOGY	SEMANTICS
0 - 3 weeks	--	Crying	Capable of producing front vowel sounds	--
3 wks. - 5 mos.	--	Pseudocry, cooing	Vocal cords changing to allow greater variety of sounds	Communicates pain, anger, hunger
6 mos.	--	Babbling, multisyllables	P, M, A	Uses holophrases
1 yr.	3 words	First words often "MaMa" or "PaPa," repetition of syllables	T, K, G, I, U	Holophrastic dictionary
2 yrs.	270 words*	Holophrastic speech, telegraphic speech, negative sentences, Wh– questions, 2–3 word (MSL)**		Addition of sentence dictionary
3-4 yrs.	1,500 words*	"ing" and "ed" verbs, "to be" verb forms (copula), negative sentences, interrogatory sentences, inflections 3-4 (MSL)**	B, M, W, H, D, N, G, NG, Z (as in azure), th (as in thick)	Addition of word dictionary; sentence dictionary partially remains
4-5 yrs.	2,500 to 3,000*	Major rules of language now acquired, complex sentences, rhyming, 4+ (MSL)**	V, R, CH, J, SH (as in shut)	Horizonal language expansion*
5 - 6 yrs.	4,000 to 5,000*	Imbedded sentences, "play" (pun) sentences, "if" and "so" clauses	F, L, HW, ZH, TH (as in that)	Semantic clusters*
6 - 7 yrs.	23,000 at end of 7th year.*	Imbedded sentences, iteration, sentence structure similar to to adults, 5+ (MSL)**	Full mastery of 44 phonemes, continues to learn rules of phonology	Vertical language expansion*

* Limited research in area indicated
** MSL = Mean sentence length

163

Linguists use three major components in analyzing language: syntax, phonology, and semantics.

Syntax. This term is used to describe the way in which words are put together to form phrases, clauses, or sentences. Children begin to babble around six months of age and say their first word about one year.

About 1½ to 2½ years of age the child begins to utter two and three word sentences. These sentences are referred to as "telegraphic speech" since they do not usually contain prepositions, conjunctions or the articles of speech. As with a telegram, only the essentials of speech are used. For example: "Me paint," "doggie bark," "all gone juice," "pretty shoes," "all fall down," and "daddy, bye bye." Between 2½ to 4 years of age the child acquires more competence in terms of sentences. Templin (1957), found the average length of sentences (mean length of sentences, MLS) from about 4.1 words to 4.7 words. (See Table 9.1.) In addition, the child begins to develop and refine verbs. (Example: "ing" and "ed" verb forms appear. "He running fast," and "I feeled the rabbit.") The child also begins to use connecting verbs (the form of the "to be" verbs — the *copula*) to link subject and predicate. (Examples: "Daddy *is* here!" "That's mine!") One can also observe the use of negative sentences ("Tommy no hit Sue." "I didn't did it.") and interrogatory sentences. "Where ball go," "Billy like spinach?" or "Why teacher crying?"

Between four and seven years of age, the child's sentence structure becomes more complex and he begins to "enjoy" language. The four year old may use a sentence containing a main and subordinate clause. Later in this period (5-7 years) the child will begin to use "if" and "so" clauses. The child now has sufficient mastery of language and may compose "pun" sentences ("Are you eating, Miss Eaton") and short poems ("I went to the zoo . . . and I saw you!") or iteration ("A rose, is a rose, is a rose . . .")

By the end of the second grade most children possess a language structure somewhat akin to that of an adult. Generally, however, they do not understand the exceptions which can occur in certain rules of grammatical construction.

Phonology. The term, phonology, is used to describe the sounds used in language. Irwin (1948) found that infants uttered sounds which could be reliably observed during the first hours of life. Usually by the end of kindergarten or first grade, the child will be able to duplicate all of the sounds in initial, medial, middle and final position.

The direction of phoneme development during the first year is from the front of the mouth to the back for vowels (ex.: a, i) and from the back of the mouth to the front for consonants. (ex.: k, g, x). However, by six months of age —when babbling occurs — the first meaningful utterances consist of a front consonant (p or m) and a back vowel (a). Thus, the first word the infant utters is usually "pa pa" or "ma ma."

According to Jakobson (1941), the sequence of phoneme development is invariant and universal. A checklist for assessing phoneme acquisition can be found in Pflaum-Conner (1978, p. 93). The reader is also referred to McNeill (1970, a) for a thorough discussion of phonology.

Semantics. The term, semantics, refers to the development of meaning. The progression of language meaning is closely related to cognition. Initially children use words holophrastically. In infant speech a "holophrase" refers to using a single word or a phrase to express a sentence-like meaning. For example: "papa" may mean, "I see daddy" or "Daddy is in bed — and I see him." McNeill (1970, a) points out that the child develops a "holophrastic dictionary." The "dictionary" is, of course, cumbersome since the infant, may pair a specific word to several meanings and is susceptible to ambiguity. The ambiguity can be reduced when the child creates a "sentence dictionary." In a sentence dictionary a word is paired with a single sentence interpretation. With additional experiences, however, the sentence dictionary likewise becomes too burdensome for the child. At this point, according to McNeill, the child moves to construct a "word dictionary."

The move to a "word dictionary" necessitates a complete reworking of the child's semantic system. In the holophrastic stage, the child stores undifferentiated information. However, with the construction of the word dictionary, the child begins to elaborate a system of semantic features.

For example: When the child is at the state of constructing the holophrastic or sentence dictionary, he may learn the word, "doggie." Since the child has no other word for animals, the child will utter "doggie" whenever he sees a cat, horse, cow, etc. At a later stage, with the acquisition of the word dictionary, the child will observe that "The *dog* is an *animal;* the *cat* is an *animal;* a *horse* is an *animal."*

In learning a language the child must learn the attributes which belong to a given concept as well as the attributes which do not belong. This process is known as *horizontal vocabulary expansion.* (McNeill, 1970, b.) Most of the words a preschool child acquires are learned in this fashion. Thus, for the child to acquire a fixed meaning for a term he must learn a dog has hair, four legs, a tail — but not whiskers, it does not say "meow," it cannot contract its claws, etc.

As the child learns the specific attributes for a concept (dog) he also masters other related concepts (cat, lion) and forms a word group (animal). This word grouping (animal) is called a *semantic cluster.* Having derived a semantic cluster, it is fairly easy to add additional concepts (horse, guinea pig, cow) to this grouping. McNeill (1970, b) has referred to this process as *vertical vocabulary expansion.*

Analyzing and extending language.

In order to help children in the development of language the writers believe that teachers of young children need to provide children with a wide variety of direct experiences utilizing a large number of materials. The teacher needs to give children an opportunity to touch, explore, and ask questions about the material. In addition, the teacher should be alerted to helping youngsters observe and discover the salient features of a given concept as well as helping them determine ways a concept differs from other related items. For example: The teacher could show children several items of fruit and discuss the attributes of the category "fruit." In this way the children can observe the fruit as an enjoyable food, and taste the fruit to determine if it is sweet or tart. The children can also discuss ways in which fruit is used — for example, as a dessert or a snack. The teacher could also help children observe differing characteristics between specific fruits in terms of color, size, texture and taste.

Nimnicht, McAfee, and Meier (1969, p. 44), presented five levels of language to help the teacher analyze language needs:

Level 1: The child is able to use a few nouns and pronouns. He needs help in the use of verbs and adjectives.

Level 2: The child uses phrases including a noun with modifiers. He needs help with verbs.

Level 3: The child uses phrases with a noun and verb —but the verb is not in agreement. Help needed to extend and refine the use of verbs.

Level 4: The child can use simple sentences, but needs help with conjunctions, negatives and possessives.

Level 5: The child can perform at level four but needs help with prepositions and concepts related to spatial relations.

The authors have found these five levels of language useful in generally assessing language development in the young child. In addition, Pflaum-Conner (1978, pp. 66-82), has constructed a sentence test and checklist which provides the teacher with a more comprehensive assessment of language development. A useful discussion is also included in terms of language as used by major minority groups in this country.

One cannot talk about cognition without discussing language development since language is virtually the only vehicle the teacher has to assess cognitive thought. Language promotes thought and develops in conjunction with cognitive growth. The writers feel it is incumbent upon the teacher to create a teaching environment which promotes and encourages language development. In the next section a number of practical suggestions are presented which will help the teacher provide many enriched experiences in the area of language.

Promoting Language Development[1]

Long before children arrive on the scene, teachers must carefully plan and structure the physical arrangement of the room, develop the daily plan of activities, and prepare herself intellectually, psychologically, and emotionally for the children.

The teacher must be a sound model and an attentive listener who speaks in a well-modulated, pleasing voice with clearly enunciated words and complete sentences. It is particularly important for teachers of very young children to speak with distinct, exacting word pronunciation and slowly enough to be easily understood. It is also essential that she use grammatically correct sentence structure. Young children use catchy phrases, "creative" mispronunciations, and word substitutes; e.g., "too early up" for "I got up too early"; "windshipers" for "windshield wipers"; "bow-wow" for "dog" and "mistappeared" for "disappeared." It is tempting for adults to pick up on the "cute" sayings of children and use them. However, this practice makes the learning of language more difficult for children who hear immature speech reinforced by the teacher.

Immature speech such as "Me getted dressed", "Me dood it", "Me go school", can be valued by adults for its place in the developmental sequence of language, but should not be reiterated by them. It is important to remember that every utterance an adult makes in the presence of children is potentially a model for speech and language development.

In order for children to feel the freedom to speak, they must feel accepted by the adults and the peers in the group. In addition, they should feel good about themselves and be secure in the acceptability of their speech. Teachers can accept immature speech patterns without reinforcing them with their own speech. Acceptability of speech becomes particularly important when teaching children whose natural language is a dialect or in some way not harmonious with "standard" English. When a child's

---

[1]This section was written by Ms. Sue Miller, former Director Early Childhood Learning Center, Columbus College, Columbus, Georgia.

168

speech is rejected, ridiculed, or constantly corrected by the teacher, he soon learns that the safest position is one of silence. Unfortunately in elementary levels it is all too often the practice to place children who move from a geographical area with a strong dialect, such as the Deep South, to an area where that dialect is not standard, into speech therapy sessions.

Children need to know that their words are important. Acceptance of the child's natural language and attempts to understand it are important for both the child and his parents.

Promoting Self Concept.

1. *Greeting.* Greet each child with his own name and a sincere, warm comment. "Good morning, Jack. I like your new brown shoes." "I'm so glad to see you, Sara. We missed you yesterday and are glad you are feeling better."

2. *Name songs and fingerplays.* Teachers who feel the freedom to improvise can make up endless songs using children's names; e.g., Tune: "Ten Little Indians."

Sherry Brown is resting quietly,
Sammy Johnson is resting quietly,
Cherish Miller is resting quietly.
I like the way you're resting.

Include songs and fingerplays like, "Where Oh Where is Pretty Little Suzie?", "Mary Wore a Red Dress", "Two Little Dickie Birds", "Muffin Man", . . . substituting children's names. In addition to using the children's names many concepts can be developed with name songs; e.g., colors, action words, street names.

3. *Puppets for dialogue.* Often children who are too insecure to speak are able to do so through puppets.

4. *Tape recorders* often intrigue children and may be a means of drawing out a shy child. Teachers may record stories, monologue or dialogue with a child. Children can learn to operate a simple cassette recorder. Shy or insecure children may find this a more comfortable situation for

talking, and verbal children may expound upon language learnings going into great detail to tell about an event or story.

5. *Provide individual locker space* with name and picture of each child. Refer to each child's space specifically.

6. *Encourage parents* to speak directly, specifically, and frequently to their child using complete sentences.

Adult-Child Interaction.

1. *Full responses.* Ask questions which illicit full responses rather than "yes" and "no" answers.

2. *Verbal interaction.* Develop skill on guiding, problem-solving, describing, reasoning, and remembering rather than dispensing abstract verbal information. Sugggestions:

a. Feel box with familiar objects.

"How does the object feel?" If more help is needed, ask, "Does it feel hard or soft?"

b. "Amy's mother is our special visitor today. If Amy's name is Amy Thompson, what is her mother's name?"

c. Encourage children to express their feelings verbally, honestly, and openly. (Teachers need to be ready to positively cope with the explosive terminology!) Teachers may frequently need to help children unravel and label their feelings. The child who is able to engage in verbal aggression, even name-calling, is making progress in language and social development.

Aggressive behavior is natural and normal in young children and peer conflicts arise quite naturally as children move from parallel into associative play. To begin to work together, accommodate ideas, agree on roles and progression of play, plan together and give in, even slightly, is difficult for children who are developmentally still caught in the throes of egocentric behavior. As conflicts arise a child's first reaction is to strike out physically. When he is able to strike out verbally he has, indeed, made progress in social development. The teacher's next task then becomes to help supply socially acceptable avenues for verbal aggression. The process is long and arduous and cannot be expected to be learned rapidly. Indeed listening to adult conversation readily portrays the fact that it is never completely achieved.

Frequently it falls to the teacher to help the child identify and label his feelings. "I know you are feeling very angry with me right now." It is quite acceptable to have negative feelings. It does not follow, however, that negative behavior should be condoned. "I know it made you mad when Billy took your truck, but I will not let you hit him."

3. *Allow children verbal opportunity.* Often adults anticipate the child's request and prematurely provide the desired item or answer, or they respond to another adult's direction to the child to verbalize; e.g. "Tom, ask Ms. Brown to pass the crackers to you." It then becomes important for Ms. Brown to wait for the child's verbalization rather than responding to the adult-child instruction.

4. *Force talk if child has language facility.*

a. "I don't understand what you want when you scream. (Even if you do understand.) Use words so I will know what you want."

b. "Sara does not know what you want when you scream, Billy. Ask her to please get off of your puzzle."

5. *Positively reinforce desired behavior.* Behavior can be reinforced by adult language; e.g., "I like the way you parked the tricycle in the garage, Billy. That is exactly where it belongs." "Good, Billy, I know just what you want when you ask me to pass the juice." "Thank you, Sara, for doing such a super job cleaning up the kitchen." "That's great Sammy. You remembered to lift the toilet seat before you used the bathroom."

6. *Verbal games.* The game of Twenty Questions can encourage verbalization of participants. In the game the leader chooses an object he is thinking of and the participants attempt to discover what that object is by asking no more than twenty questions. The game can be varied to suit the age level of the group.

Other description games can be developed by creative teachers; e.g., "I am thinking of something in the room which is bright blue." Let children guess, modify your statement. "Now, I am thinking of something in the room which is bright blue and round." The game can greatly enhance descriptive vocabulary. After getting the idea the children can give each other clues and continue the guessing game.

Language Opportunities.

There are a variety of opportunities for language during the daily schedule of events. The writer feels that communication, both verbal and non-verbal, should be sincere, honest, and meaningful.

This is, by no means, an exhaustive list of language experiences, but suggestions to spur the reader's thinking about the vast array of continuous opportunities which sometimes go unnoticed. It is the writer's hope that as teachers observe and interact with children daily, they will become more cognizant of the many opportunities for language stimulation and vocabulary development.

1. *Snack time.* Snack time offers an excellent opportunity for casual conversation and the incorporation of many language skills. The reader is reminded of how closely language and concept development are bound. Suggestions:

a. Use the child's name at snack time.

b. Plan coordinating menus, when possible, to allow for concepts of food processing, classifications of foods, and varied forms of the same fruit; e.g., serve raisins and grape juice; apples and apple juice; lemon slices and lemonade; make peanut butter using peanuts, salt and oil in a blender; serve milk and let each child shake his own butter using a small portion of cream in a baby food jar; cook cranberries and serve cranberry juice; taste raw pumpkin when making jack-o-lanterns and use cooked pumpkin for a pie or toast the pumpkin seeds.

c. Discussion at snack time can center upon the shapes, colors, and tastes of snack items and table service. For example: napkins, cups, color of juice and snack item, shape of items, taste of food stuffs, substance on the outside of crackers, pretzels, sugar cookies.

d. Use the conversational opportunity for building memory skills; e.g., important events in child's life — the new doll; learning to ride a bike; his trip to the barber shop;

172

a trip taken on vacation; what we saw yesterday when we visited the farm; your favorite thing to do outside; your favorite part of the fair.

e. Memory skills can be further fostered by questions like: "Yesterday was Amy's birthday. Do you remember what she brought for birthday treat?" "I really am hungry. It's been a long time since breakfast. What did you have for breakfast this morning, Amy?"

f. The conversational atmosphere of snack affords the opportunity to discuss seasonal changes occurring including names of seasons and weather terminology. "Was it hot or cold when you came to school this morning? Is it sunny, rainy, cloudy, snowy, windy? How can you tell it is Fall?"

g. Snack is a natural place to integrate other areas of curriculum. Discussions can occur about where foods are grown, how they grow, where we buy them, how the grocer obtains foods, what we grow in our garden, where milk comes from and numerous other aspects of science and social studies.

h. Adults are usually most conscious of manners at snack time. Like other aspects of language and social skill development, children learn most effectively from our actions. Be a good example of manners. If the important adults in the child's environment say "please," "thank you" and "excuse me" children will learn good manners also. Be aware, too, of how often adults are not only impolite but rude to children in their attempts to force proper etiquette.

2. *Calendars.* Calendars can be used for number concepts and sequence of days and months, and also for looking ahead and anticipating special events and talking about plans; e.g., vacations, birthdays, holidays, and remembering past special events this month.

3. *Story time.* Stories are an excellent means of stimulating language experiences. It has been the experience of the writer than when group story time immediately preceeds free play there is a far greater tendency for the children to use the flannel board figures, scrolls, puppets, and charts, and books to retell the story for themselves and interested peers, and to discuss the story than when story time is presented prior to snack, music, or outdoor play.

If teachers use props such as puppets and flannel board figures in the story presentations, children are also more inclined to use these materials.

It is important to vary the method of storytelling to maintain interest in story time and to attract and stimulate individual children. Too often, unfortunately, teachers cursorily select a book from the shelf just for the sake of having a story. If one of the purposes of story time is to create an interest in books and an enjoyment of reading and hearing stories, it is imperative that the teacher carefully plan in terms of story selection and method of presentation.

Some books lend themselves especially well to the verbal participation of children; e.g., *Are you my mother?*[1] — "The baby bird walked and walked and pretty soon he came to a _____." Let the children supply the name of the animal. Many books contain repeated phrases which allow children to supply the words. For example: "Run, run as fast as you can; you can't catch me, I'm the Gingerbread man."

Teachers sometimes neglect the use of poetry with children. Poetry is valuable not only as a source of literary enjoyment, but also as a means of recognizing like word endings. Teachers often fail to respond to the cues a child gives in his attempt to recognize similar word endings and nonsense rhyming. It is not uncommon to hear children exploring language and cueing into auditory likeness through such nonsense word play as "Tommy-wommy;" "You're a stupid-woopid" and later such taunts as "Sue Ellen looks like a melon."

4. *Music.* Music provides an excellent opportunity for language development through repeated use of words and phrases. Memory skills are extended and children are repeatedly given the opportunity to use language. Short songs with simple tunes and repeated phrases are especially well suited for mastery by young children. Music time can be varied by using musical instruments, picture cards

---

[1]Eastman, P. D. *Are you my mother?* New York: Beginner Books, 1960.

to cue the next verse, or flannel board figures. Suggestions:

a. Instruments. Voice tones are easier for young children to match. However, occasionally using an instrument can add zest to singing; e.g., ukulele, guitar, autoharp, kalimba, resonator bells, xylophone, piano, recorder, or computer.

b. Picture cards. Songs like "Hush Little Baby", "Fair Rosie", and "There Was an Old Lady Who Swallowed a Fly" are especially well suited for picture card clues.

c. Flannel board. Flannel board figures also give excellent cues particularly if prior characters are incorporated with each new verse; e.g., "The Little White Duck", "Old MacDonald", "She'll Be Comin' 'Round the Mountain", "I Had a Little Rooster by the Barnyard Gate."

d. Movement. Movement songs and records provide many vocabulary word introductions and may be used to reinforce concepts; e.g., body parts, clothing, high, low, up, down, backward, forward, fast, slow, rolling, jumping, hopping, etc. Songs of this type are available through song books and numerous movement and concept records.

5. *Water table.* Many direct experiences can be provided at the water table, but the quality of the learning taking place is dependent upon the quality of the teacher-child interaction. Concepts such as solution, full, too full, half full, empty, sink, float, dissolve, bubble, whip, fill, drain, etc. can be expanded upon and vocabulary can be extended encompassing the activities.

6. *Art.* Conversation during the art experience can be expanded by helping the child to describe the color, shape, size, texture, smell, and occasionally taste of the media. The teacher should be cautioned not to dictate the process of the creation. For example, comments can be made about color blends, brush strokes, pictorial representations (if the child in that developmental stage without directing the process.) Children's voluntary verbalizations can be recorded on the back of the picture. Joseph and Marilyn Sparling (1973) discuss how a teacher can converse meaningfully with children involved in art, particularly those in the scribbling stage.

7. *Housekeeping.* The housekeeping area is a natural center for children to converse together. It allows children

the opportunity to play various roles, solidifying ideas and making concepts real to them. Teachers need to encourage children to talk with each other without unnecessary adult interference. Suggestions for the housekeeping area:

a. Provide areas for kitchen, dining room, store, etc.

b. Provide ample time for children to freely express themselves.

c. Provide "dress up" clothes like ladies' hats, high heel shoes, scarves, and party dresses.

d. Provide suitable containers or storage areas which foster classification skills: a place for hats, shoes, handbags, jewelry, doll clothes, silverware, dishes, pots and pans, empty boxes and cans of food stuffs.

e. Provide special props for role playing particularly if interest in the area is waning: play dough, dry macaroni, rice, dry beans.

8. *Blocks.* Blocks can serve many purposes. Language, math, social studies are all reflected in the block area. The following incident vividly portrays the importance of role-playing and of the teacher's language in learning and reinforcing concepts.

The children had established a lumberyard using the unit blocks for their wares. The teacher approached the clerk (a four year old child) and said, "I would like to buy two long rectangle blocks." The clerk got the requested items for the customer. "Thank you," the teacher responded. "How much money do I owe you?" The four year old clerk looked at the blocks and very deliberately counted, "One, two. That will be two dollars." The teacher carried through the role and pretended to give the clerk two one dollar bills. In a few minutes the teacher returned to make another purchase. "I would like to buy one long rectangle block and two medium size rectangle blocks," she stated. The child filled the order correctly and the customer said, "How much money do I owe you?" Once again the child very deliberately counted the items. "One, two, three. That will be three dollars." "Oh," said the teacher, "But these two medium-size blocks are the same length as one long block," as she carefully placed the two shorter blocks beside the longer block. With a studied look on his face the four year old clerk restated, "These two blocks *are* the same as one long block." He stood silent for a moment pondering the situation then moved his finger first down the two shorter blocks then down the long block saying, "One, two," and very happily replied with a broad smile, "That will be two dollars!"

Concepts such as high-low; long-short; same-different; and relative sizes can readily be incorporated into block play. Other concepts can be developed with the addition of props such as puppets, small wheel toys, animal and human figures.

9. *Bulletin board and concept area.* Bulletin boards and concept tables can effectively spur communication and cognitive development. While areas should be changed often enough to stimulate interest, they should remain the same for a period of time which is sufficient enough to allow for exploration, expansion and solidification of concepts. It is important that the concept table include concrete, realistic objects for children to manipulate. Sufficient symbolic representation can be accomplished on an eye-level bulletin board. For example, if the concept to be emphasized is big and little, the teacher can prepare a "Big and Little" bulletin board. Large and small objects, a magnifying glass, reducing lens, books and flash cards can be placed on the concept table.

10. *Cooking.* Even very simple cooking experiences like making chocolate milk and cinnamon toast provide numerous opportunities for discussion. Social studies concepts can be discussed as one examines the importance of food and the food chain. Occupations connected with growing and distributing food are interesting areas to explore. Science experiences include sensory perception, the changing of matter and the effects of heat and cold.

Pictorial recipe charts can be made for recipes which involve measuring ingredients. For very young children the charts should be large and designed so children can "read" the pictures to determine how many cups of a particular ingredient are required. Words and numerals are also used on the chart. Older children who have developed reading skills can gradually read more and more words. By third grade youngsters may be able to manage cooking experiences with very little help from the teacher, using recipes printed on large file cards.

The addition of a recipe chart extends cooking activities to include language arts and math curriculum areas. As in every teacher-planned activity, the quality of learning will depend largely upon the skillful questioning techniques of the teacher. For example:

a. "We have all of the ingredients and equipment which we need to make cookies. Which ingredient do we need to put into the bowl first?"

b. "How many cups of sugar do we need to measure into the bowl?" Proceed through the recipe chart in the same manner.

c. "What do you think will happen to the sugar when we put in the eggs?" "Does the sugar still look dry?" "What made the sugar become wet?"

d. "Now our cookies are all ready to bake. Can you still see the sugar (referring to sugar container) in the cookies? Why can't we see it?"

e. "Are the cookies ready to eat now? What else do we need to do to them?" If the children are unable to respond with the idea of baking, the teacher provides the term and shows them where things are baked.

f. As children are preparing to consume the tasty morsels, use the opportunity to review the ingredients used to make the cookies.

g. Cooking is truly an integrated curriculum experience. Concept areas and skills included in cooking are sequencing, ordinal position, numerals, measurement, ingredients, changing mass, effects of heat or cold, where ingredients are purchased, where and how they grow, how ingredients taste, how a finished product smells and tastes, exposure to printed words, and memory.

11. *Field Trips.* Field trips can be an optimal opportunity for enhancing language development, vocabulary expansion, and concept areas. Field trips must be carefully planned by the teacher and the site visited prior to taking the children. For example:

178

a. The teacher must communicate to the adults involved the importance of structuring their speech in understandable terms for children.

b. Talk with the children about expected behavior on the trip. For example, what to do if the fire alarm rings while visiting the fire station; staying seated in the bus; holding hands to cross streets.

c. Discuss what the children will be seeing. Introduce and explain some of the anticipated new experiences. For example, the role of the veterinarian; smells and places where smells might be located; the dentist's chair that goes up and down; the railroad tracks in the roundhouse; being quiet in the library.

d. Anticipate possibly frightening aspects of the trip; e.g., the loud noise of jack hammers; the size of cows (some children have been close to cows and some have only seen them from a distance).

e. Follow-up conversations about what was seen, heard, smelled, special tools, titles or professions of people visited, the child's favorite part of the trip, or other appropriate topics.

f. Listen carefully to what children say and correct possible misconceptions. The writer is reminded of the reaction of a four year old boy who refused to drink milk after visiting a dairy farm stating, "That cow done peed the milk."

12. *Special visitors.* It is often difficult for professional persons to discuss their jobs in simple, understandable terms. Prior to their visit, the teacher should talk with the visitor and explain the level of concepts which are to be discussed.

This difficulty is vividly portrayed by the teacher who invited a banker to talk with her second grade class during a unit on money. The children were immediately confused as he spoke in terms of simple and compound interest, prime interest rate, principal, mortgages, and investments. She was particularly uncomfortable when the banker began to pass ten, twenty, fifty and one hundred dollar bills to the children for examination.

179

The writer is also reminded of the frightful experience when a fireman visited a three year old nursery group. Endeavoring to be dramatic he produced a model house and proceeded to demonstrate very vividly how the house caught on fire, and as it appeared to burn, how the people were trapped inside.

The teacher needs to know exactly what the visitor plans to do. It may be necessary for her to play a primary role in asking appropriate questions.

13. *Holidays.* The celebration of holidays can be an exciting event for teachers and children. Frequently it is a time when children abound in enthusiastic verbalization. Many language opportunities also avail themelves in music, fingerplays, stories, art, trips, and special events. However, it is important for the teacher to remember the child's concept of temporal relationships and keep the period of celebration short.

14. *Outdoor Activities.* The same activities which promote the use of language by children and the same techniques of communication are applicable out of doors as well as inside the classroom. For example:

a. "Good, Billy. You have climbed all the way to the third knot."

b. There are an endless supply of concepts available to the teacher: Back and forth on the swing; forward and backward on the trikes; up and down the hill or see-saw; down the slide; inside the tunnel; up the tree house; swinging and riding fast and slow; running; jumping; ways to cross the balance beam; rough and smooth rocks; wet grass; splashy puddles; pouring and measuring sand or water; hard concrete, soft grass; tall trees, short bushes.

c. Awareness of weather and seasonal changes. Weather effects our daily lives. Children are always hearing adults talk about the weather. There are many concepts which are appropriate for discussion with youngsters. Hint: TV weather personalities often enjoy coming to a school to discuss the weather. Usually these persons are trained in the use of techniques which can make weather concepts meaningful and entertaining.

d. Planting, caring for and harvesting the products of the school garden. There is tremendous excitement in watching a seed break through the ground as a small plant. Harvesting carrots or pulling a peanut plant from the ground will cause even the most hesitant child to burst forth with enthusiasm.

It is often a temptation for the teacher to seize outdoor play time as her chance to sit quietly, relax and converse with other teachers — making certain only that fights are stopped and safety is maintained. Careful observation, however, will show that many opportunities arise for teacher to capture the teachable moment and promote language.

Summary.

While the roles of communicator and active listener are important, the writer urges teachers to consciously spend time objectively and systematically observing children. Through such attentive observation teachers receive valuable information about how children initiate conversations, the quality of speech and language development as well as social, emotional, physical and cognitive development, concepts and misconcepts which have been obtained and concepts of self in all areas of life. Through observation, it may become obvious to a teacher that a child's self-concept is very positive and secure in one area but ineffectual and negative in another. For example, he may feel quite secure dealing with cognitive tasks yet very insecure in a social context; he may be comfortable with adults but unsure with peers; he may feel very confident in reading and fearful of math.

Careful, sensitive observation, coupled with other evaluative processes, makes it possible for teacher to adequately plan for the optimal development of each child.

It is not enough to have the finest equipment available and supplies in sufficient quantity, to have a beautiful physical environment in which to teach, to have exquisitely formulated behavioral objectives and logical sequencing of developmental tasks, and a perfectly balanced schedule of events, though all of these are important. It is not enough for the teacher to have a thorough understanding of child growth and development and be able to formulate excellent written plans, and to possess the necessary paper credentials and certificates to teach children, though these must not be underestimated. The ability to make practical application of theory, to be responsive to the needs of the individual children in the group, and to effectively communicate with each child is essential. The quality of learning taking place in the classroom is directly related to the ability of the teacher to structure her language in a manner which will stimulate and guide children's thinking and stimulate and promote their use of language.

It is through the effective use of language that the teacher can truly integrate curriculum and continually reinforce concepts. It is the writer's belief that the essential element in teaching is the quality of the warm, responsive interaction between teacher and child.

CHAPTER TEN

Educational Implications

When teachers understand cognitive development they can use this information to help plan their curriculum. If teachers are cognizant of how children acquire knowledge they can determine the most appropriate subject matter material for the class and for the individual child. They can also decide when and how to introduce material in the most efficient manner. Piaget provides a systematic perspective for understanding and interpreting how children develop. A working knowledge of Piagetian theory can help teachers plan and evaluate effective teaching strategies.

Piaget's work has a number of implications for the educator. Several key features in his theory can provide the teacher with a *frame of reference* for observing and understanding the children she teaches. As mentioned several times in this text, we believe that Piaget's greatest contribution was his observation that children view their world differently than adults. The manner in which they establish rules and moral codes and their method of organizing thought is unique to childhood. This chapter will briefly examine the goals of early childhood education in relation to Piagetian theory. We will also provide several guidelines for the teacher and demonstrate some implications for educators through the practical application of cognitive theory.

Goals of Early Childhood Education.

While the thrust of Piagetian theory focuses on a major goal in education, i.e., the acquisition of knowledge; the reader should be aware of other goals which are also vitally important to the child's total development. Education can, of course, have many goals. Most educators would include the ability to think and reason, the acquisition of knowledge and vocational skills, the development of personal, social and moral values. Education should help a person become a better adjusted, more fulfilled individual who can function as an effective, contributing member of society. In his work, Piaget did not actually address himself to the goals of education, *per se*. Piaget said simply, "The ultimate goal of education should be the development of people who are creative, inventive, and discoverers."

According to Forman and Kuschner, two major proponents of Piagetian theory, the purpose of early childhood education is the construction of knowledge in order to improve the quality of life. A good education should provide the student with the means to construct and use knowledge effectively and to develop the skills necessary to construct intelligence from scattered facts. Through education the student should become happier, more interested and more aware. Almy (1982, p.3) states, "The overarching goal for the preschool curriculum that is based on Piaget's theory is to support the development of each child's intelligence, or knowledge."

However, some critics would view the goals of education differently. They would emphasize the teaching of facts in a "pressure cooker curriculum." Under these circumstances a major goal is to teach materials faster and quicker, and to speed up the teaching process. Piaget termed this phenomenon, "the American Question." That is, "How can we 'speed up' the developmental process and teach concepts faster?" "What 'shortcuts' can we develop which will teach certain concepts at an earlier age?" Piaget has stated that only in the United States is he asked how cognitive development can occur "sooner" and "quicker." Rather than establishing a "quickie curriculum," we believe the goal of education should be to insure that each child has the opportunity to develop his own intellectual and social skills and abilities as fully as possible.

Guidelines for the Teacher.

1. **Administer the cognitive tasks developed by Piaget.** In terms of the Piagetian tasks, *per se,* we feel there are many

advantages for the teacher. Our experience has shown that as teachers actually administer the cognitive tasks which are presented in this text, they *immediately* begin to enlarge their understanding of children and the way they think. We cannot overemphasize this point — the actual administration of the tasks provides a "hands on" experience which is invaluable in gaining insight into the processes involved in cognition. We believe that this approach gives teachers a new frame of reference. By developing a comprehensive knowledge of the tasks and through the utilization of Piaget's unique method of questioning, the teacher is equipped with a better understanding of the way children solve problems and look at the world. As the teacher increases her own knowledge of cognitive development, we believe she will alter her approach to children and enrich her own philosophy of teaching.

To some extent the tasks are competency based and the teacher can diagnose and construct a "plan of action" for each child. Knowledge of the child's thinking helps the teacher to identify the child's cognitive level. She knows the level at which the child appears to be operating, and the gaps in his ability to reason logically. The teacher can then provide concrete experiences and materials which will encourage further development.

2. **Recognize the perceptual difference in reality.** As we have seen, the child is not a miniature adult. Moreover, he possesses a unique mental structure which is *qualitatively* different from older persons. Thus, the child's conception of reality is fundamentally different from the adult's perception of reality. We have also seen that the preoperational child is egocentric and believes that others see the world *exactly* as he does. He selectively *centers* on certain attributes of a problem and he attends to "states" rather than transformations. He cannot reverse his thoughts and seems incapable of symbolic manipulation.

During the preoperational period a child may count to ten without making an error. Some adults will believe that the youngster has mastered the concept of number. Yet, as we have seen in some of the cognitive tasks presented in this book, a child may believe that a set of five buttons contains more than a set of seven buttons, if the physical arrangement of the set is altered. The teacher of young children must quickly learn that the preoperational child often uses words which possess a different meaning than the usual adult connotation. A three year old may say, "We share here!" but then be totally unable to share. Even elementary children in the early stages of concrete operations will use terms which have little or no meaning for them. Many adults believe that once a child has learned a "label," he understands the underlying concept. *Children learn their vocabulary from adults, but the meanings are derived from their own unique experiences.*

Ginsburg and Opper (1979, p. 223) summarize the educational implication for these perceptual differences:

> . . . the educator must make a special effort to understand the unique properties of the child's experience and ways of thinking. The educator must try to adopt a child-centered point of view, and cannot assume that the child's experiences or modes of thinking are his own. For example, while the educator himself may learn a great deal by reading a book or listening to a lecture, similar experiences may be far less useful for the child. The educator may profit from an orderly sequence of material, but perhaps the child does not. While the educator may feel that a given idea is simple and indeed self-evident, the child may find it difficult. In short, it is not safe to generalize from the adult's experience to that of the child. The educator's assumptions, stemming as they do from the adult perspective, may not apply to children. The educator needs to improve his own capacity to watch and listen, and to place himself in the distinctive perspective of the child. Since the meaning expressed by the child's language is often idiosyncratic, the adult must try to understand the child's world by observing his actions closely.

3. **Learning takes place through the process of construction.** Earlier in the text we noted a very important premise in Piagetian theory. Piaget hypothesizes that: Knowledge is not passively received from the environment but actively constructed by the individual. Piaget believes that children construct their conception of the world via *active* involvement with material objects and people.

Children do not change their beliefs overnight or as a result of "being told." Rather they change and alter their perceptions *gradually* and over a period of time. This fact —the acquisition of knowledge over time — leads to the notion that intelligence is constructed. For example: The neonate may be exposed to his bottle several hundred times. Yet if the bottle is presented to him with the blunt end first, he will not know what to do with the bottle because he has not "constructed" the object in his mind. Usually, sometime during the eighth month, the infant will recognize that the bottle has a reverse side and turn the bottle to the nipple end. Thus, by the eighth month the child has learned, via construction, that the bottle has two ends.

4. **Activity is a vital part of cognitive development.** Research suggests that most concepts cannot be meaningfully acquired without related activity. Piaget has said that it is necessary for children to have concrete experiences in order to form their own hypotheses and verify them through their own active manipulations. Children do not learn effectively through the passive process of absorption and osmosis. The teacher should provide a number of learning experiences which allow and encourage children to actively engage in the process of manipulation and discovery. Piaget said, "To act is to know."

Ginsburg and Opper (1979, p. 225) state, "Teachers can in fact impose very little knowledge. It is true that they can convince the child to *say* certain things, but these verbalizations often indicate little in the way of real understanding. Moreover, it is seldom legitimate to conceive of knowledge as a *thing* which can be transmitted." Yet, in spite of these research findings many teachers attempt to teach pre-operational children difficult concepts via pictorial representations and through passive experiences. Lectures and verbal bombardment may result in a surface type of learning in which the child can state the correct response without understanding the nature of the response. *For young children the most effective learning settings require activity and concrete experience.*

Please note: This guideline is not meant to suggest that youngsters do not need to achieve representational competence. As Sigel and Cocking (1977) and Copley, *et al*, (1979) have shown, representational competence is a vital part of cognitive development and can be effectively utilized in an early childhood curriculum. In addition, Piaget (1969, p.68) once noted, " . . . while the child's activity at certain levels entails the manipulations of objects . . . at other levels the most authentic activity may take place in the spheres of reflection, of the most advanced abstraction and of verbal manipulations, provided they are spontaneous and not imposed on the child."

Rather, the point being emphasized here is the importance of activity in the mastery of cognitive concepts. Unfortunately, some teachers tend to believe that lectures, drills, workbooks and other vicarious experiences are the *only* components necessary to a learning environment.

5. **A challenging environment is a vital part of cognitive development.** Children need activity — but they also need stimulation and caring. They need adults who will provide enriched experiences which will challenge them to explore their environment. The teacher needs to establish a setting which is challenging to the child and which can provide many enriched experiences. The reader is referred to the wide variety of language experiences suggested in Chapter Nine.

The major difference in the Piagetian classroom is not the material, *per se*, but the way in which the environment is structured and the way the teacher perceives the learning climate. As the teacher gains knowledge of the child's abilities (to think logically), his general developmental level, it helps her to determine the incongruities in the curriculum. For example, the teacher of two to three year old children can recognize the child's sensori-motor interests, his limited vocabulary, and his feelings of egocentricism. Knowing this, the teacher would not empha-

size sharing and cooperative play, but rather provide a wide variety of concrete experiences in the sensori-motor area.

The kindergarten teacher likewise recognizes the limitations of the five to six year old. Using the concept of time as an example: the teacher recognizes that terms like "ten o'clock" or "eleven forty-five" have little meaning to the child. "Ten o'clock" has meaning when the teacher relates it to "snack time." "Eleven forty-five" is related to "lunch time." The concept of tomorrow is understood in terms of "after you go to bed at night and get up the next morning."

The teacher must analyze and evaluate activities and materials to determine the possibilities inherent in regular curriculum areas. For example, blocks have been popular since the inception of the kindergarten. The Froebelian teacher used blocks to teach the unity of God and man. Patty Hill blocks were used to build barns and forts. Kindergarten unit blocks became roads, cities, and towns. The teacher who understands the Piagetian philosophy will utilize blocks in ways which promote cognitive growth and development. Let us examine some of the experiences which can be provided by block building.

Why Have Block Building?

a. *Creativity:* Block building is a relatively unstructured activity. Blocks can be used in as many ways as the imagination allows.
b. *Motor Coordination:* Gross and fine.
c. *Teach relational concepts:* For example: Over, under, beside, next to, on top of, etc.
d. *Classification skills:* Group by classes: Large blocks, small blocks. Fractions, 1 to 1 correspondence. Label block shelves by block type.
e. *Conservation:* Concept of gravity. "The blocks will fall." Concept of weight. "What do I need to balance this side?" Concept of length. Learning that blocks are invariant.
f. *Spatial Relations:* As tall as, taller than. "Can you find two blocks that are equal to this long block?" "Will the fire engine fit inside the building?" Learning that two objects cannot occupy the same

190

space at the same time. Thinking in the third dimension.

g. *Temporal Relations:* "After block time." "You have a lot of blocks and it will take you a long time to pick them up." "How long did it take to build this structure?"

h. *Problem solving:* "We are out of cylinder blocks; what else can we use?"

i. *Vocabulary building:* Relational concepts, spatial concepts. New words like: cylinder, ramp, bridge, tunnel, tower, structure.

j. *Sequencing:* First, second, third. "Big blocks at the base; small blocks at the top."

k. *Social development:* Group play, exploring various roles, sharing and taking turns, limits, rules.

l. *Values:* Clean up, respect for property rights, sharing, limits.

Routine tasks and activities can assume new meaning. The teacher should study and analyze the various aspects of her curriculum. For example an analysis of snack time suggests the following:

Goals for Snack Time

a. Food intake.
b. New foods for cultural enrichment.
c. Vocabulary (discussing how things taste, feel, appear).
d. Classification skills (food, dishes, colors, people).
e. Conservation of quantity.
f. Fine motor coordination.
g. One-to-one correspondence (one napkin and one glass per person.).
h. Spatial relations (pouring, position of glass).
i. Temporal relations (before and after juice).
j. Manners (through modeling).
k. Values (sharing, wasting, clean up).
l. Socialization.

The examples given are illustrative of ways the teacher can take curriculum areas and activities and examine them in a systematic fashion to determine their *raison d'etre*. In their book Copple, Sigel, and Saunders (1979) present an in-depth analysis of the teacher's role in a Piagetian curriculum. They specifically show how teacher strategies, planning and evaluation can occur when utilizing a Piagetian frame of reference.

6. **Understand the sequence of learning concepts.** For years a child's ability to recite numerals 1, 2, 3, 4, etc. was considered a basic skill in mathematics and when a child had difficulty the traditional answer was, "He will just have to sit and memorize . . . " The child learned to add and subtract via rote learning and it made little difference if he understood how he arrived at an answer as long as it was correct. The study of cognitive development demonstrates that there is much more to mathematics than mass memorization. For example, before a child can adequately use and understand the abstract numeral for "seven" he must be able to:

Learning the numeral, "seven"

a. Understand one-to-one correspondence.
b. Count one by one.
c. Understand the concepts "more than," "less than," and "as many as."
d. Understand the concept of reversibility. (Seven less one is six; seven less two is five; seven less five is two, etc.)
e. Understand the components of "seven," i.e., what combinations of other numbers when combined yield seven? (one & six; two & five, etc.)
f. Understand the invariance of a given number.
g. Recognize, identify and relate a number to each symbol.

Kamii and DeVries (1980) have suggested a number of group games as a vehicle for the utilization of Piagetian theory. In their book, *Piaget, children and number,* these authors show how the teacher can foster the development of early numerical quantification. Forman and Kushner (1977) have conducted several creative experiments with children through the utilization of some equipment not usually found in early childhood programs. For example they use pendulums, rollers, dowels and pipes. Copple, *et al,* (1979) employ a number of regular classroom materials. Their suggestions to the teacher concerning the "importance of focus" and the value of inquiry provide valuable insights for workable teacher strategies. However, as Almy (1982, p.4) so aptly states, "In general, the major difference between the Piagetian and other classrooms lies in the teachers' thinking about the ways the environment can affect children's actions and their thought."

7. **Utilize the "scientific method".** Earlier in this text we mentioned the use of the scientific method in working with young children. This approach could also be designated the "problem solving" paradigm or design. By the scientific method we mean that children should be encouraged to: a) question and hypothesize, b) test the hypotheses, c) observe the results, d) draw generalizations, and e) revise the original hypotheses in terms of the findings. Copple, *et al* (1979) discusses the problem solving approach in detail and provide many excellent examples. Their chapter on science is particularly helpful to the teacher of young children.

8. **Recognize the child's cognitive style.** As we saw in Chapter Two, the manner by which persons perceive, interpret, and respond to a given situation can vary greatly. Kagan (1964) and Sigel (1972) have referred to this approach as one's *cognitive style.* Two children may make the same score on an I.Q. test and yet be quite different when it comes to problem solving and conceptual ability. Messer (1976) found that by five to six years of age, a child's cognitive style is fairly stable and changes relatively little over time. Information on the child's cognitive style can be helpful to the teacher as she plans learning strategies for each individual child. The simple test item provided in Chapter Two gives the teacher an indication of the child's style or approach to a problem. (Note: Of course, the results of a single test item should not be taken as the sole evidence for the youngster's approach to problem solving.) The teacher should observe the child in other settings to gain additional infomation on his learning style.

The research in this area suggests that some children tend to be impulsive; others reflective in their approach to problem solving. Impulsive children tend to blurt out the first thing which comes to mind; they act impulsively and give little thought to a problem. In reading aloud, impulsive youngsters may "hurry" over their words. The result is that the child skips words, substitutes the incorrect word and/or mispronounces a word. The impulsive child often takes the easiest approach to a problem and fails to consider other alternatives or implications. Research suggests that hyperactive children tend to be impulsive.

Reflective children tend to be more precise and exacting in their approach to problem solving. They are more analytic and usually take more time to consider the various alternatives before deciding on a definite course of action. In addition to the test item presented in Chapter Two, Malcolm, *et al,* (1982) have developed a scale which will measure learning styles. Two researchers, Egeland (1974) and Heider (1971), offer some suggestions for ways to work with these children.

9. **Utilize the "method clinique".** Through this technique, the *method clinique,* Piaget was able to discover what children thought, how they reasoned and how they reached conclusions. Through his method of inquiry Piaget discovered that children think differently than adults. He also found that children may think differently at different ages and stages of development.

For example, suppose we were to ask the following question to a group of children: "Which weighs more, a pound of feathers or a pound of steel?" A four year old would not understand the question and reply, "I don't know." A seven year old would say, "The steel weighs more because it is heavier." A twelve year old would respond, "Since a pound is a standard measuring unit, they both weigh the same."

In this example Piaget would examine both the correct and incorrect response of youngsters. He was often more fascinated with the incorrect answer since it provided insight into the child's manner and level of reasoning ability.

In utilizing the *method clinique,* the investigator is not so concerned with the child's lack of specific information — rather the researcher is interested in how the child reasons about a problem. This information reveals how a child thinks — and how he thinks is the product of his developmental level.

The central core of Piaget's research strategy was his use of questioning and requestioning. We see this approach in the cognitive tasks which are presented in this book. By utilizing this technique, the teacher can gain tremendous insight into children's modes of thinking. In too many instances, however, teachers inhibit the questioning process by telling youngsters, "You are incorrect," or "That will not work!" This type of negative reasoning only serves to discourage children and may cause them to terminate an activity. The teacher should encourage questions and, in some instances, introduce discrepancies which would challenge children to think through problem situations. The teacher will find the following suggestions helpful:

a) **Use questions as a technique for gaining information.** All too often teachers do not listen to children. Remember President Lyndon Johnson's admonition, "When you are talking you are not learning anything!" As you listen to youngsters, be prepared to ask questions which will help you to understand their activities.

b) **Ask questions in a direct, yet simple manner.** Use terms and words which children can easily understand. Keep your questions clear and succinct.

c) **Use open-ended questions.** Ask questions which permit children to respond in several ways. Open-ended questions allow youngsters to examine several possibilities rather than searching for the "one" correct response.

d) **Ask questions which will encourage problem solving behavior.** Ask questions like, "I wonder what would happen if . . . ?" or "Which colors would go well with that box?" "What would happen if all the children wanted the same chair?" Questions can help the child to predict future actions and consequences and begin to learn problem solving strategies.

e) **Ask questions which show you are interested.** Remember that children model their behavior after the teacher. Help children observe the advantages and sheer joy of asking questions and seeking answers. Let your comments show the child that you are interested in his activity.

f) **Use "How" questions rather than "Why" questions.** In many instances young children do not understand casuality and connections between events may be totally unrelated. For example the teacher may get responses like, "Turning on the light makes the train go." "Touching the stick made Theron jump." Generally, "why" questions are unproductive. Ask children to pay attention to actions and their effect — e.g., the "how" question.

g) **Record both the correct and incorrect response.** As mentioned earlier, the incorrect response can serve as a diagnostic tool for determining the child's level of thinking.

h) **Probe and requestion.** If the teacher is unclear on the child's response, she should probe further and ask the question in a different way. Piaget points out that the technique of requestioning enables the interviewer to probe more deeply into the child's thinking. In many instances the child will clarify or amplify his reasoning when asked additional questions.

A Curriculum based on Piagetian Theory.

In implementing the goal of helping children construct and develop knowledge, Almy (1982) states that four factors should be taken into account. The curriculum should: a) Allow for the differing rates of maturation in children (individual differences). b) Provide opportunities for children to act on the physical environment. c) Provide opportunities for social interaction. d) Foster self-regulation by allowing as much autonomy as possible.

Within the past few years several authors have addressed themselves to designing a curriculum based on the theories of Piaget. It is not the goal of this text to detail these curricula, nor to describe the role of the teacher as viewed by the various program designers. However, these projects are, for the most part, well conceived and detailed in such a manner that the individual teacher will profit by an intense examination of the different programs. A complete reference is contained in the bibliography.

Three programs have been developed that contain a number of facets which are directly attributable to Piagetian theory. These programs are all practical and workable and we believe the teacher can garner many ideas from an examination of the curricula. The programs do vary in terms of approach and teacher role. However, all are quite explicit and will provide the teacher with many useful suggestions that can apply to her own situation. The book by Copple, *et al,* discusses the advantages of developing representational competence and provides the most detail in terms of specific curriculum areas like art, music, and science.

Biber, B., Shapiro, E., & Wickens, D. *Promoting cognitive growth: A developmental-interaction point of view.*

Copple, C., Sigel, I., & Saunders, R. *Educating the young thinker: Classroom strategies for cognitive growth.*

Hohman, M., Banet, B., & Weikart, D. *Young children in action: A manual for preschool educators.*

There are two programs which follow Piagetian principles more closely and tend to be more theoretically oriented. However, both programs are well designed in concept and have many practical and realistic suggestions which teachers can implement in their own program. Four books are suggested below. These books detail the two programs and provide the teacher with useful ideas. Forman and Kushner's books provide practical suggestions for learning encounters and Kamii and DeVries utilize group games which can (1980, p. xi) " . . . stimulate children's development in unique ways if used with the insights gained from Piaget's theory." Earlier in this chapter we mentioned the book by Kamii and DeVries concerning children and number.

Forman, G., & Kushner, D. *The child's construction of knowledge: Piaget for teaching children.*

Forman, G., & Hill, F. *Constructive play: Applying Piaget in the preschool.*

Kamii, C., & DeVries, R. *Physical knowledge in preschool education.*

Kamii, C., & DeVries, R. *Group games in early education: Implications of Piaget's theory.*

Finally, we believe that understanding cognitive development and the administration of the Piagetian tasks will alter and enrich the teacher's philosophy. We believe this approach gives teachers a new "set" when observing children. It enriches and makes the questions she asks more meaningful. We feel the teacher can attain proficiency which permits daily, ongoing evaluation of her group.

We also feel that this theoretical framework provides the teacher with the "ammunition" she often needs to defend her program and her philosophy to administrators, other teachers, curriculum coordinators, and parents. Piagetian theory helps the teacher plan curriculum; the tasks help her to diagnose the intellectual status of her children and set meaningful goals. Through reappraisal, the teacher can determine if these goals have been met.

Appendix A

COGNITIVE TASKS PROTOCOL

NOTE: The protocol form in Appendix A and the illustrations in Appendix B may be obtained in a larger size (8½″ x 11″). For price and order information, write directly to the publisher.

COGNITIVE TASKS
PROTOCOL

Child's Name: _____ Date of Birth:_____ Age:_____

Examiner: _____ Date(s) of Examination:_____

Teacher: _____ Classroom:_____

Set I — PERFORMANCE SUMMARY

CONSERVATION (Tasks 1-12)

1. Length	UC	T	NH
2. Distance	UC	T	NH
3. Quantity	UC	T	NH
4. Area	UC	T	NH
5. Number:			
a) as many as	UC	T	NH
b) bunched	UC	T	NH
6. Number:			
a) 1:1 correspondence	UC	T	NH
b) more than	UC	T	NH
c) less than	UC	T	NH
7. Number & Space	UC	T	NH
8. Counting	UC	T	NH
9. Regrouping	UC	T	NH
10. Additive relations	UC	T	NH
11. Height	UC	T	NH
12. Volume	UC	T	NH

CLASSIFICATION (Tasks 13-20)

13. Simple classification			
a) graphic collection	UC		NH
b) chaining	UC		NH
c) eight groups	UC		NH
d) four groups	UC		NH
14. First dichotomy	UC		NH
15. Second dichotomy	UC		NH
16. Third dichotomy	UC		NH
17. Seriation-sticks	UC	T	NH
18. Seriation-balloons	UC	T	NH
19. Class Inclusion I	UC	T	NH
20. Class Inclusion II	UC	T	NH

TEMPORAL RELATIONS (21-24)

21. Time & Space	UC	T	NH
22. Age	UC	T	NH
23. Time, measurement I	UC	T	NH
24. Time, measurement II	UC	T	NH

SPATIAL RELATIONS (25-29)

25* Straight line			
a)	UC	T	NH
b)	UC	T	NH
26* Position location I	UC	T	NH
27* Position location II	UC	T	NH
28. View of face			
a) back	UC		NH
b) right	UC		NH
c) left	UC		NH
d) front	UC		NH
29* Water level	UC	T	NH

* Reproduce child's response on protocol (Page 2).

201

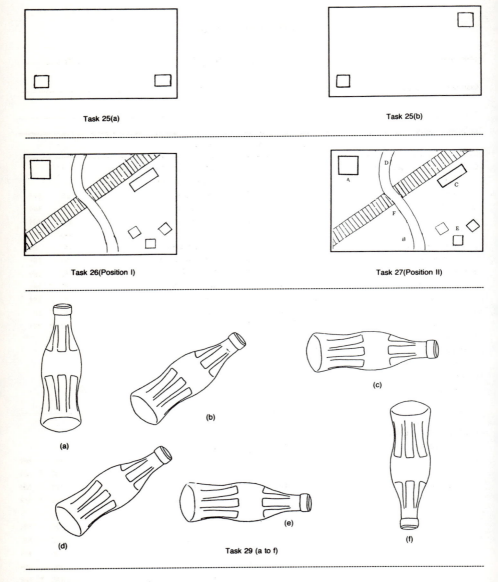

Task 25(a)

Task 25(b)

Task 26(Position I)

Task 27(Position II)

Task 29 (a to f)

Reproduce child's responses on protocol.

202

REASONING SKILLS (Tasks A - G)

A The best buy:
1.   UC   NH
2.   UC   NH
3.   UC   NH

B Fractions:
1.   UC   NH
2.   UC   NH
3.   UC   NH

C Time and distance:
1.   UC   NH
2.   UC   NH
3.   UC   NH

D Age problems:
1.   UC   NH
2.   UC   NH
3.   UC   NH

E Prediction problems:
1.   UC   NH
2.   UC   NH
3.   UC   NH

F Proverbs (Note: record child's
response in observation notes.)
1.   UC   NH
2.   UC   NH
3.   UC   NH
4.   UC   NH
5.   UC   NH
6.   UC   NH

G Syllogism: UC   NH

MORAL DEVELOPMENT (Tasks H, I, J, K)

(Note: Refer to Chapters 2 and 8. There is no scoring of UC, T, or NH for these tasks. The examiner should record the child's responses and the reasoning for the judgements made. These replies should be included in the observation notes.)

GENERAL OBSERVATIONS: Answer specific items. Use additional pages for observation notes:

1. How did the subject relate to the examiner? _____

_____

2. Did subject perseverate? (Experience difficulty in moving to new tasks?) _____

3. Cognitive Style: (See chapter 2.) Circle: R   I

4. How did subject react to apparent success? Apparent failure? _____

_____

_____

5. If frustrated, how did the subject react? _____

_____

_____

203

6. Special observations in terms of vocabulary _____

_____

7. Did subject evidence visual problems. _____

8. Did subject appear to hear clearly? Use normal voice? Did instructions need repeating? If so, how often? _____

_____

9. How did subject's general approach to the tasks compare with the rest of the group?

_____

_____

OBSERVATION NOTES: (Use additional pages for observation notes, as necessary.)

Appendix B

ILLUSTRATIONS FOR COGNITIVE TASKS

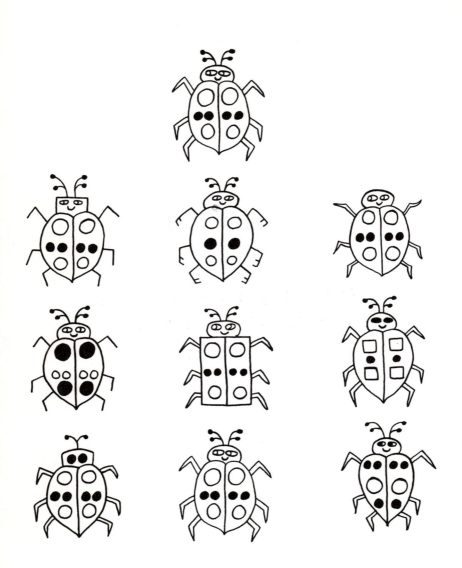

Model for Test of Cognitive Style. See discussion in Chapter Two.

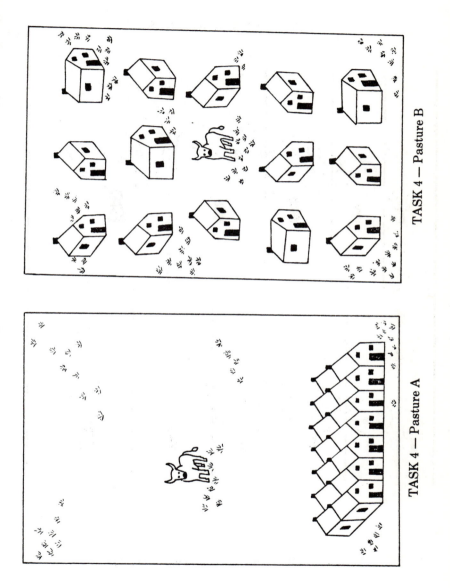

TASK 4 — Pasture B

TASK 4 — Pasture A

207

P 1 P 2 P 3 P 4 P 5

A 1 A 2 A 3 A 4 A 5 A 6

MODEL FOR TASK 22: Apple and Pear Trees.

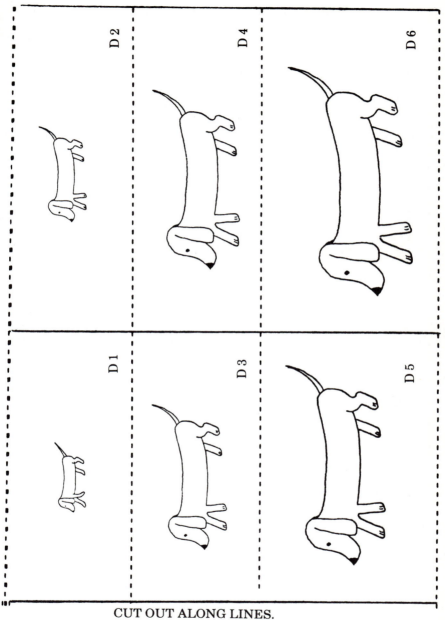

CUT OUT ALONG LINES.

Model for Task 22 . . . Dachshunds

CUT OUT ALONG LINES.

Model for Task 22 . . . Irish Setters

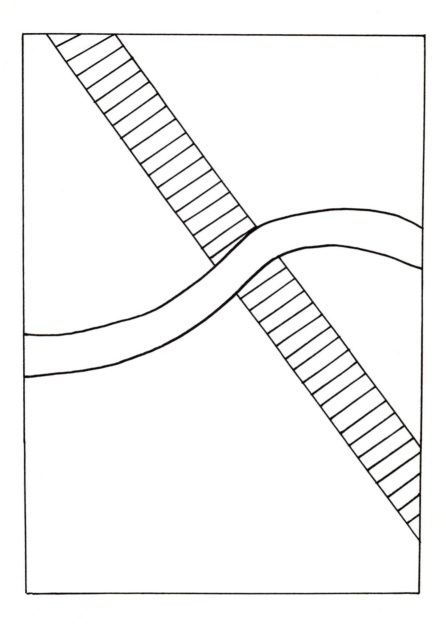

Model for Task 26 and Task 27. (Note: Two landscapes needed.)

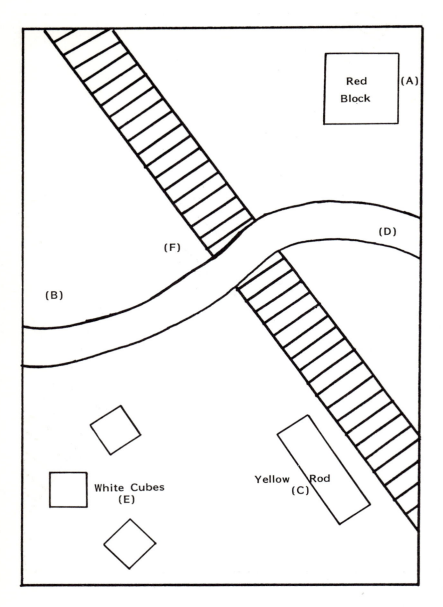

Key for Tasks 26 and 27. (Note: Positions for the man in Task 27 are labelled: A, B, C, D, E, and F.)

TASK 28 — Situation A

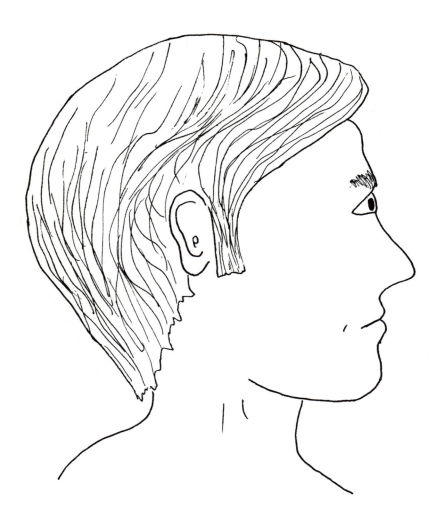

TASK 28 — Situation B

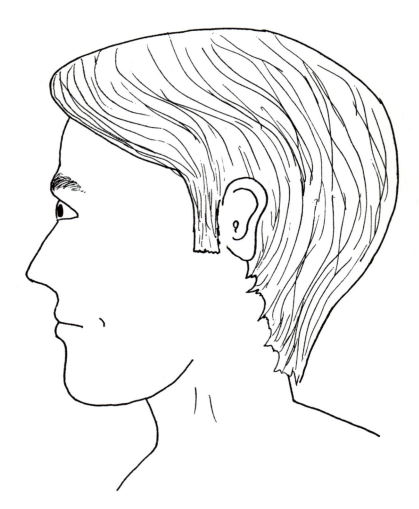

TASK 28 — Situation C

TASK 28 — Situation D

218

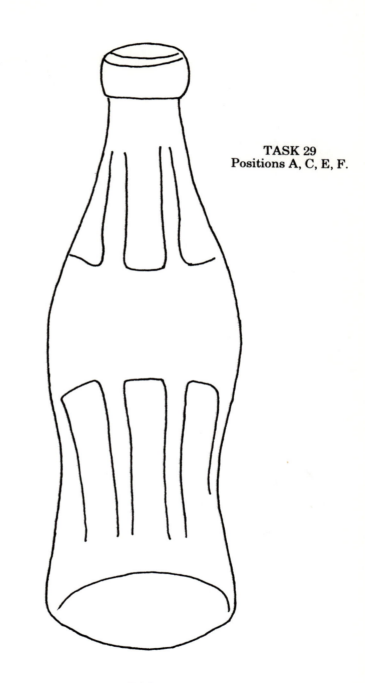

TASK 29
Positions A, C, E, F.

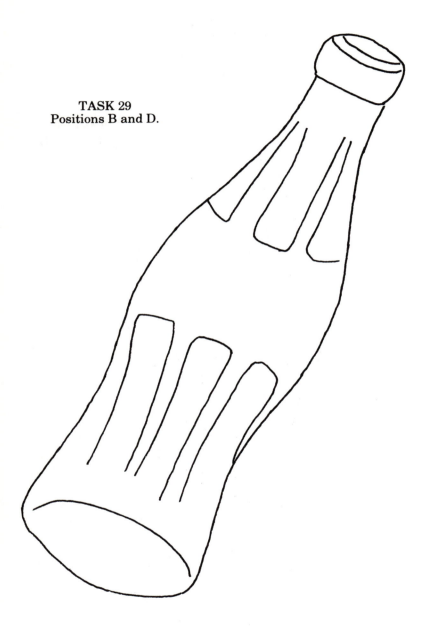

TASK 29
Positions B and D.

Appendix C

SAMPLE PROTOCOL — "OCIE T."

COGNITIVE TASKS
PROTOCOL

Child's Name: _Ocie T._ Date of Birth: _9/10/75_ Age: _7:04 yrs._

Examiner: _Michelle A. Hendrickson_ Date(s) of Examination: _1/10; 1/12; 1/14/83_

Teacher: _M.A. Hendrickson_ Classroom: _2B_

Set I — PERFORMANCE SUMMARY

CONSERVATION (Tasks 1-12)

1. Length — UC T (NH)
2. Distance — UC T (NH)
3. Quantity — UC (T) NH
4. Area — UC T (NH)
5. Number:
   a) as many as — (UC) T NH
   b) bunched — (UC) T NH
6. Number:
   a) 1:1 correspondence — (UC) T NH
   b) more than — (UC) T NH
   c) less than — (UC) T NH
7. Number & Space — UC T (NH)
8. Counting — (UC) T NH
9. Regrouping — UC T (NH)
10. Additive relations — UC T (NH)
11. Height — UC T (NH)
12. Volume — UC (T) NH

CLASSIFICATION (Tasks 13-20)

13. Simple classification
    a) graphic collection — UC (NH)
    b) chaining — UC (NH)
    c) eight groups — UC (NH)
    d) four groups — UC (NH)
14. First dichotomy — (UC) NH
15. Second dichotomy — (UC) NH
16. Third dichotomy — (UC) NH
17. Seriation-sticks — UC (T) NH
18. Seriation-balloons — UC (T) NH
19. Class Inclusion I — UC T (NH)
20. Class Inclusion II — UC T NH

See observation notes!

TEMPORAL RELATIONS (21-24)

21. Time & Space — (UC) T NH
22. Age — UC (T) NH
23. Time, measurement I — UC T (NH)
24. Time, measurement II — UC (T) NH

SPATIAL RELATIONS (25-29)

25* Straight line
    a) — UC (T) NH
    b) — UC (T) NH
26* Position location I — (UC) T NH
27* Position location II — (UC) T NH
28. View of face
    a) back — (UC) NH
    b) right — UC (NH)
    c) left — UC (NH)
    d) front — (UC) NH
29* Water level — UC T (NH)

---
* Reproduce child's response on protocol (Page 2).

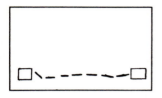

Task 25(a)

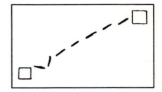

Task 25(b)

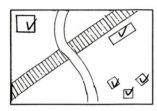

Task 26(Position I)

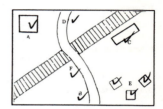

Task 27(Position II)

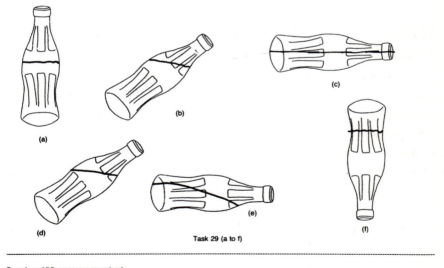

(a)

(b)

(c)

(d)

(e)

(f)

Task 29 (a to f)

Reproduce child's responses on protocol.

223

REASONING SKILLS (Tasks A - G)

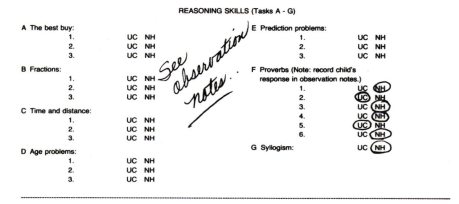

A The best buy:
1.   UC NH
2.   UC NH
3.   UC NH

B Fractions:
1.   UC NH
2.   UC NH
3.   UC NH

C Time and distance:
1.   UC NH
2.   UC NH
3.   UC NH

D Age problems:
1.   UC NH
2.   UC NH
3.   UC NH

See observation notes.

E Prediction problems:
1.   UC NH
2.   UC NH
3.   UC NH

F Proverbs (Note: record child's response in observation notes.)
1.   UC **(NH)**
2.   **(UC)** NH
3.   UC **(NH)**
4.   UC **(NH)**
5.   **(UC)** NH
6.   UC **(NH)**

G Syllogism: UC **(NH)**

MORAL DEVELOPMENT (Tasks H, I, J, K)

(Note: Refer to Chapters 2 and 8. There is no scoring of UC, T, or NH for these tasks. The examiner should record the child's responses and the reasoning for the judgements made. These replies should be included in the observation notes.)

GENERAL OBSERVATIONS: Answer specific items. Use additional pages for observation notes:

1. How did the subject relate to the examiner? *Ocie T. was very excited and wanted to do the tasks because Derek had told her about doing the "games."*

2. Did subject perseverate? (Experience difficulty in moving to new tasks?) *No. Ready to move on to next task.*

3. Cognitive Style: (See chapter 2.) Circle: **(R)** I

4. How did subject react to apparent success? Apparent failure? *She would usually hesitate and try to figure out the correct answer before giving the examiner an answer.*

5. If frustrated, how did the subject react? *She was quite excited over her success and a good sport about her failures. She really took the failure well.*

6. Special observations in terms of vocabulary *In some of the tasks I had to change the wording.*
   Ocie did not always understand. Her vocabulary seems about average for this age.

7. Did subject evidence visual problems. *None*

8. Did subject appear to hear clearly? Use normal voice? Did instructions need repeating? If so, how often? *She seemed to hear clearly. Used a normal voice. Instructions did not need repeating.*

9. How did subject's general approach to the tasks compare with the rest of the group?
   Ocie was not as talkative as other children tested. She is very attentive, however.

OBSERVATION NOTES: (Use additional pages for observation notes, as necessary.)

Ocie T. was not very talkative. She does pay attention and seems to be reasonably motivated. I felt that she did her best on the tasks. Ocie did not volunteer any additional information on the tasks and usually did not comment further unless I asked her a direct question. She appears to be an average student in terms of the others in the class. However, after observing her in the classroom setting and after administering the tasks, I do believe she could profit from some additional experiences. She enjoys playing games and I plan to make up some games which can relate to her school work. I have already talked with Ocie's mother and she has indicated that she would be happy and willing to play some games with Ocie which might provide some additional experiences.

1/16/ 83.

Name: Ocie T.   Date: 1/14/83

Task 1: Conservation of Length

When Ocie lined the two rods along side of each other, she said that they were
the same length. When I moved one of the rods about one inch ahead of the
other rod, she said that the one I moved was the longest. I asked why? She
hesitated and said, "because you moved it!" I do not think she quite understood
this concept and needs help in this area.

Task 2: Conservation of Distance

Ocie appeared confused on the conservation of distance. When the task was
presented to her she observed the blocks close together and then moved them
far apart. When asked what she had done, she said that she moved the blocks
away from each other all the way to the edge of the table. After the book had
been placed between the blocks, she said that the blocks were now "closer
together."

Task 3: Conservation of Quantity

Ocie is clearly in transition in terms of the conservation of quantity. When I
asked her if the balls of clay were the same, she held them in her hands for
awhile and then agreed that they were the same. Then I rolled one ball into
a hot dog. Ocie said they were the same and then said, "No the hot dog is
bigger." I requestioned as follows: E: "Are you sure?" O:"Yes...(hesitates)
No...Yes!"

Task 4: Conservation of Area

The task was a bit confusing to Ocie. She could not conserve area after three
houses were added. She said, "I have never lived on a farm -- so I really
don't know much about farming." Ocie need more experience in this area.

Task 5: Conservation of Number (as many as and bunched)

Ocie seemed to understand the concepts of "as many as" and "bunched." First
she counted the circles and said that she had as many circles as she had
squares. I asked her if she was sure. She rechecked by matching one circle
with one square until she had matched each circle with a square and had no
circles left over. When the circles were bunched together I asked, Are there
as many circles as there are squares? She said, "Yes, I just counted them."

Task 6: Number (1:1 correspondence, more than, less than).

When I presented Ocie the objects she immediately said that there were as many
squares as there were circles. However, when she began to match one to one,
she said, "No, there are more circles than squares." When I asked why she
said that, she replied, "because I do not have a square to match one of my
circles, I don't have as many squares as I have circles and I need one more
square."

226

Task 7: Number & Space

In this task I arranged the buttons in my row so that my row was longer than
Ocie T.'s row. I asked, "Are there as many buttons in your row as there are
in my row?" Ocie said, "No, your row is longer than my row." Upon requestioning
it was obvious that Ocie actually thought that I had more buttons. She said,
"Can't you see -- you have more buttons, because your row is longer." In this
area, the subject is a nonconserver -- she is unable to override the perception
of length.

Task 8: Counting

Ocie appears to understand this concept. I spread the chips in front of her
and asked her to count them aloud. She counted them correctly, assigning a
name to each button. She was unable to look at the entire set and identify the
total number of elements -- but she was able to count them one-by-one. She
said, "There are seven buttons."

Task 9: Regrouping

When I regrouped the chips (I made three groups-- 2+2+3), Ocie was confused.
She began to count the buttons again. I said, "Can you tell me how many buttons
there are just by looking?" She shook her head and continued to count the buttons. When she completed her counting she announced, "There are eight buttons."
(Note: Since there are only seven buttons in the task, she had made a miscount.)
Ocie did not understand the concept of regrouping -- she need help in this
area.

Task 10: Additive Relations

When I asked Ocie if there was the same amount of cereal for both days she
said "No...that there is more cereal on the second day." As in tasks 7 and
9, Ocie is confused and does not understand the invariance of number.

Task 11: Measurement of Height

Ocie had difficulty with this task. Her tower of blocks kept falling. She could
not build the tower without help. I finally helped her hold the tower up so she
could continue to build. Actually she became so involved in the building per
se, she neglected to keep track of measuring. When she finally completed her
tower, she picked up the ruler and attempted to make a measurement but she
was unable to use the ruler correctly. (She "played like" she was making a
measurement -- she really did not know how to use the ruler.) She looked at
me and said, "I think that your tower is bigger than mine." Ocie still needs
help with this concept -- she needs more experience with measurement.

Task 12: Volume

Ocie was confused on the task of displacing water. On the one hand, she grasped
the idea that the balls would cause displacement; but, one the other hand, she
could not use the term. (Note: I found that some of my other children did not
understand the term, "displacement" --I used the term, "just as high.") Ocie
said that the hot dog would make the water go higher. However, when she saw
the hot dog in the water she said, "I think they are the same." However, upon
requestioning, she would say -- "The hot dog is bigger." As with Task 3, Ocie
appears to be in transition.

Task 13: Simple Classification

When the situation in Task 13 was presented to Ocie, she said, "I see different colored pencils." I had to probe further to get responses on sizes and the fact that some of the pencils were sharpened. When she put the pencils that she thought went together, she seemed to have just kept color and size in mind. Help in this area would be beneficial for Ocie.

Task 14: First Dichotomy

Ocie did much better on this task than on Task 13. She grouped the pencils correctly in two bundles. When requestioned, she grouped them by color, sharpness, and length. Therefore I am omitting Tasks 15 & 16.

Task 17: Seriation -- Sticks

When I asked Ocie to place the sticks in order from the shortest to the longest at the bottom of the line, she did it by trial and error. First, she moved them all down to the line, then she looked and rearranged them. She would move the sticks back and forth -- and check one against the other. She was not exactly sure of the last two sticks, so she stood them on end to make a judgement. She left the two stick standing up (out of sequence). When asked, "Why did you lay the sticks this way?" She looked puzzled and said, "Well, this was the way you want, ain't it?" Since some of the sticks were out of sequence and because of the method used, I have checked "T" for this task.

Task 18: Seriation -- Balloons

Again the subject seriated the objects by trial and error. However, at times she would try placing the smaller balloon over the larger, just to be sure. It took a long time for Ocie to complete the task. She really remained interested, but it was quite obvious that the seriating of objects was difficult (and she did make some errors). I believe that we need to give Ocie some opportunities to work with the seriation of objects. She needs the experience and she seems to enjoy the task.

Task 19: Class Inclusion I

I asked Ocie, "Are all of these animals dogs?" She answered, "Yes." E: "Is this animal a cat?" O: "Yes." E:"Are there more dogs her or more cats?" O: "More dogs." Then I asked, "Are there more dogs here or more animals?" Ocie replied, "More dogs." When I asked why she said there were more dogs Ocie responded, "Cause I see a bunch of dogs over here ... and I see a cat by hisself right over there!" Ocie needs help in this area; she does not understand class inclusion. I did not administer Task 20.

Task 21: Time & Space

Ocie appeared to understand this concept. She answered the questions correctly and upon requestioning said that the reason her car finished first was because both cars were racing and hers was the faster car.

Task 22: Age

Ocie had difficulty with this task. When asked which tree was the oldest, she said they were both just as old. When asked why she said that it was because both trees were the same size and you get bigger when you get older. When shown the pictures of the dogs, she said that the Irish Setter was older because "That dog is bigger."

Task 23: Time measurement I

In this task Ocie thought the sand moved fastest the first time but was slower the second time. She needs help in time measurement.

Task 24: Time measurement II

Ocie predicted that the hand on the stopwatch would have been at thirty. She assumed that time was going faster because she counted faster. Ocie is not able to tell time. Sometimes during class she will ask, "Is it lunch yet?" or "Have we had lunchtime?"

Task 25: Straight Line Projection

Ocie formed a line by pointing her finger and using it as a sighting device. However, the last two posts on the far left were somewhat wavy. She used the same technique for Situation (b).

Task 26: Location of Positions I

Ocie did not have any problems with this task. She reproduced all the pictures correctly.

Task 27: Location of Positions II

Ocie really seemed to enjoy this task. She said, "This is fun. It is like playing checkers." She placed her man correctly in all six positions.

Task 28: View of Face

Ocie performed situations (a) and (d) without any trouble. She immediately stood in the correct position. When it came to positions (b) and (c), she would point her finger to the direction that the nose in the picture was facing. Then she would turn and face in that direction.

Task 29: Water Level

Ocie needs help with this concept. She does not understand spatial representation of water level. She drew and colored three correct water levels, but this was only after I had given her considerable help. (a),(c), and (d).

229

Reasoning Skills (Tasks A - G)

(Note: Since Ocie T. is only seven years of age, I did not try to administer the tasks A,B,C,D,E. Authors' Note: Most youngsters under eight years will be unable to perform tasks A - E. The examiner will need to make this decision based on the skills of the child.)

Task F: Proverbs

1. (Fight fire with fire.) "If you start fighting, someone will start fighting you."

2. (A penny saved is a penny earned.) "If you save your money, you get more. If you are smart then you will have money for things that are important."

3. (Strike while the iron is hot.) "I don't know that; I really don't know much about irons or ironing."

4. (The early bird get the worm.) "And he eats it. Do you know what that means? He chews up the worm and he swallows it." E: "But what does, 'the early bird gets the worm mean to you?' " O:"It dies?" E:"What dies?" O: "The worm!"

5. (A stitch in time saves nine.) "It means you do it real quick." E:"What happens if you do it real quick?" O: "You might not do it right."

6. (A bird in the hand is worth two in the bush.) "I don't know that one."

Task G: Syllogism

O: "That's really silly. You know that all dogs ain't red!"

Task H: Jim & Terry

"Jim was naughtier because he broke more cups. He should be punished more than Terry because he broke more cups."

Task I: The Heinz dilemma

"That one is hard. He needs the medicine for his wife, but he shouldn't steal. E: "But his wife was very sick." O: "You still shouldn't steal."

Tasks J & K: Moral Dilemmas I and II

(I) "I would help my friend." E:"How would you do this?" O: "I would just help her." (shrugs shoulders) E: "What would you do if the teacher said she wants everybody to do their own work?" O: "The teacher would help my friend. She said if we needed help to ask her." (When confronted with the dilemma, Ocie seemed to "avoid" it by saying that her teacher would "solve" the problem of the friend needing help.)   (Dilemma II) O: "The teacher would know what to do, because cheating is bad." Even when requestioned, Ocie would not pursue this -- said that the teacher would handle the problem....O: "She would know what to do."

BIBLIOGRAPHY

Almy, M. Applying Piaget's theory in the early childhood classroom. In K. Osborn (Ed.), *Resource Report.* Chicago: World Book—Childcraft, 1982.

Appel, M. The application of Piagetian learning theory to a science curriculum project. In M. Appel & S. Goldberg (Eds.), *Topics in cognitive development.* New York: Plenum, 1977.

Baldwin, A. *Theories of child development.* New York: Wiley, 1967.

Bandura, A. *Social learning and personality development.* New York: Holt, Rinehart and Winston, 1963.

Biber, B., Shapiro, E., & Wickens, D. *Promoting cognitive growth: A developmental-interaction point of view.* Washington: NAEYC, 1971.

Bowlby, J. *Maternal care and mental health.* Geneva: World Health Organization, 1951.

Brown, M., Skeen, P., & Osborn, K. Young children's perception of the reality of television. *Contemporary Education,* 1979, *50,* 129-133.

Bruner, J. (Ed.). *The developing child.* London: Fontana, 1977.

Cazden, C. Some implications of research on language development for preschool education. In R. Hess & D. Baer (Eds.), *Early Education.* Chicago: Aldine Press, 1968.

Cazden, C., *Language in early childhood education.* Washington: NAEYC, 1972.

Charles, C. *Teacher's petit Piaget.* Belmont, CA: Fearon, 1974.

Clark-Stewart, A., & Apfel, N. Evaluating parental effects on child development. In L. Shulman (Ed.), *Review of research in education.* Itasca, IL: Peacock, 1979.

Clark-Stewart, A., & Koch, J. *Children: Development through adolescence.* New York: Wiley, 1983.

Copple, C., Sigel, I., & Saunders, R. *Educating the young thinker: Strategies of cognitive growth.* New York: Van Nostrand, 1979.

Cowen, C. *Piaget with feeling: Cognitive, social and emotional dimensions.* New York: Holt, Rinehart and Winston, 1978.

Dale, P. *Language development.* New York: Holt, Rinehart and Winston, 1976.

Dennis, W. Causes of retardation among institutional children: Iran. *Journal of Genetic Psychology,* 1960, *96,* 47-59.

DeVries, R. Constancy of generic identity in the years three to six. *Monograph of the Society for Research in Child Development,* 1969, *34* (3), Serial #127.

DeVries, R. Relationships among Piagetian, IQ, and achievement assessments. *Child Development,* 1974, *45,* 746-756.

Egeland, B. Training impulsive children in the use of more efficient scanning techniques. *Child Development,* 1974, *75,* 165-171.

Elfman, J. Encouraging preschoolers' intellectual development. In K. Osborn (Ed.), *Resource Report.* Chicago: World Book—Childcraft, 1981.

Erikson, E. *Childhood and society.* New York: W. W. Norton, 1963.

Flavell, J. *The developmental psychology of Jean Piaget.* Princeton: Van Nostrand, 1963.

Forman, G., & Kuschner, D. *The child's construction of knowledge: Piaget for teaching children.* Monterey, CA: Brooks/Cole, 1977.

Forman, G., & Hill, F. *Constructive play: Applying Piaget in the preschool.* Monterey, CA: Brooks/Cole, 1980.

Frost, J. *Early childhood education rediscovered.* New York: Holt, Rinehart and Winston, 1968.

Frost, J., & Kissinger, J. *The young child and the educative process.* New York: Holt, Rinehart and Winston, 1976.

Furth, H. *Piaget and knowledge.* Englewood Cliffs: Prentice-Hall, 1969.

Furth, H. *Piaget for teachers.* Englewood Cliffs: Prentice-Hall, 1970.

Gelman, R. Conservation acquisition: Learning to attend to relevant attributes. *Journal of Experimental Child Psychology,* 1969, *7,* 167-187.

Ginsburg, H., & Opper, S. *Piaget's theory of intellectual development.* Englewood Cliffs: Prentice-Hall, 1969.

Ginsburg, H., & Opper, S. *Piaget's theory of intellectual development* (2nd ed.). Englewood Cliffs: Prentice-Hall, 1978.

Goodrow, J. Children's drawing. In J. Bruner (Ed.), *The developing child.* London: Fontana, 1977.

Havighurst, R. *Developmental tasks and education.* New York: David McKay, 1972.

Hohman, M., Banet, B., & Weikart, D. *Young children in action: A manual for preschool educators.* Ypsilanti, MI: High Scope Press, 1979.

*Inhelder, B., & Piaget, J. *The growth of logical thinking from childhood to adolescence.* New York: Basic Books, 1958.

Irwin, O. Infant speech: Development of vowel sounds. *Journal of Speech and Hearing Disorders,* 1948, *13,* 31-34.

Irwin, O. Infant speech: Effect of systematic reading of stories. *Journal of Speech and Hearing Research,* 1960, *3,* 187-190.

Jakobson, R., *Fundamentals of language.* The Hague: Mouton, 1941.

Kagan, J., Rosman, B., & Phillips, W. Information processing in the child. *Psychological Monographs,* 1964, *78,* #578.

---

*Reference by Piaget which is particularly appropriate to educators.

Kagan, J. Impulsive and reflective children: Significance of conceptual tempo. In J. Krumboltz (Ed.), *Learning and the educational process.* Chicago: Rand, McNally, 1965.

Kamii, C., & DeVries, R. *Physical knowledge in preschool education.* Englewood Cliffs: Prentice-Hall, 1978.

Kamii, C., & DeVries, R. *Group games in early education.* Washington: NAEYC, 1980.

Kellogg, R. *Analyzing children's art.* Palo Alto: Mayfield, 1970.

Kelly, M. *The developmental acquisition of Piagetian concepts of identity in young children.* Unpublished doctoral dissertation, The University of Georgia, 1979.

Kohlberg, L. The development of children's orientation toward a moral order: Sequence in the development of moral thought. *Vita Humana,* 1963, *4,* 87-94.

Kohlberg, L. Stage and sequence: The cognitive-developmental approach to socialization. In D. Goslin (Ed.), *Handbook of socialization theory and research.* Chicago: Rand-McNally, 1969.

Kohlberg, L. The cognitive-developmental approach to moral education. *Phi Delta Kappa,* 1975, *46,* 670-677.

Kohlberg, L., & Maier, R. Development as the aim of education. *Harvard Educational Review,* 1973, *42,* 449-496.

Lavatelli, C. *Piaget's theory applied to an early childhood curriculum.* Boston: American Science & Engineering, 1970.

Leeper, S., Skipper, D., & Witherspoon, R. *Good schools for young children.* New York: Macmillan, 1979.

Lennenberg, E. *Biological foundations of language.* New York: Wiley, 1967.

Maier, H. *Three theories of child development.* New York: Harper & Row, 1978.

McCelland, D. Testing for competence rather than for intelligence. *American Psychologist,* 1973, *28,* 1-14.

McNeill, D. The development of language. In P. Mussen (Ed.), *Carmichael's Manual of Child Psychology.* New York: Wiley, 1970. (a)

McNeill, D. *The acquisition of language.* New York: Harper & Row, 1970. (b)

Messer, S. Reflection-impulsivity: A review. *Psychological Bulletin,* 1976, *83,* 1026-1052.

Malcomb, R. *The learning style identification scale.* East Aurora, NY: Slosson, 1982.

Nimnicht, G., McAfee, O., & Meier, J. *The new nursery school.* New York: General Learning, 1968.

Osborn, K. *Early childhood education in historical perspective.* Athens, GA: Education Associates, 1980.

Payne, B. Moral development: You and your child. In K. Osborn (Ed.), *Parent's Viewpoint.* Chicago: World Book—Childcraft, 1982.

Phillips, J. *The origins of intellect: Piaget's theory.* San Francisco: W. H. Freeman, 1969.

*Piaget, J. *Language and thought in the child.* London: Kegan Paul, 1926.

Piaget, J. *The child's conception of the world.* New York: Harcourt and Brace, 1929.

*Piaget, J. *The psychology of intelligence.* London: Routledge, 1950.

*Piaget, J. *The construction of reality in the child.* New York: Basic Books, 1954.

Piaget, J. *The moral judgement of the child.* New York: Macmillan, 1955.

Piaget, J. *The child's conception of space.* London: Routledge, 1956.

Piaget, J. The child and modern physics. *Scientific American,* 1957, *196* (3), 46-57.

*Piaget, J. *Play, dreams and imitation in childhood.* New York: Norton, 1962.

*Piaget, J. *Science of education and the psychology of the child.* Middlesex, England: Penguin, 1969.

Piaget, J. *The child's conception of movement and speed.* London: Routledge & Kegan Paul, 1970. (a)

Piaget, J. *Genetic epistemology.* New York: Columbia Univ. Press, 1970. (b)

*Piaget, J. An autobiography. In R. Evans (Ed.), *Jean Piaget: The man and his ideas.* New York: Dutton, 1973.

Piaget, J., & Inhelder, B. *The child's construction of space.* New York: Norton, 1948.

*Piaget, J., & Inhelder, B. *The psychology of the child.* New York: Basic Books, 1969.

Pflaum-Conner, S. *The development of language and reading in young children.* Columbus, OH: Merrill, 1978.

Robison, H., & Schwartz, S. *Learning at an early age* (2 vols.). Englewood Cliffs: Prentice-Hall, 1972.

Roeper, A., & Sigel, I. Finding the clue to children's thought processes. In W. Hartup & N. Smothersgill (Eds.), *The young child.* Washington: NAEYC, 1967.

Schwebel, M., & Raph, J. *Piaget in the classroom.* New York: Basic Books, 1973.

Sigel, I. The attainment of concepts. In M. Hoffman & L. Hoffman (Eds.), *Review of child development research.* New York: Russell Sage Foundation, 1964.

Sigel, I., & Hooper, F. *Logical thinking in children.* New York: Holt Rinehart and Winston, 1968.

Sigel, I. The development of classificatory skills in young children: A training program. In W. Hartup (Ed.), *The young child: Reviews of research.* Washington: NAEYC, 1972.

Sigel, I., & Cocking, R. *Cognitive development from childhood to adolescence.* New York: Holt, Rinehart and Winston, 1977.

---

*Reference by Piaget which is particularly appropriate to educators.

Singer, D., & Revenson, T. *How the child thinks*. New York: New American Library, 1978.

Skeels, H., Updegraff, R., Wellman, B., & Williams, H. A study of environmental stimulation: An orphanage preschool project. *University of Iowa Studies in Child Welfare*, 1938, *15*, #4.

Skodak, M., & Skeels, H. A final follow-up study of one hundred adopted children. *Journal of Genetic Psychology*, 1949, *75*, 85-125.

Smith, E., Goodman, K., & Meredith, R. *Language and thinking in school*. New York: Holt, Rinehart and Winston, 1976.

Sparling, J., & Sparling, M. How to talk to a scribbler. *Young Children*, 1973, *28*, 33.

Templin, M. *Certain language skills in children*. Minneapolis: University of Minnesota Press, 1957.

Vygotsky, L. *Thought and language*. Cambridge: M. I. T. Press, 1962.

Wadsworth, B. *Piaget's theory of cognitive development*. New York: Longman, 1979.

Weikart, D. *The cognitively oriented curriculum*. Washington: NAEYC, 1971.

Weisberg, P. Social and nonsocial conditioning of infant vocalizations. *Child Development*, 1963, *34*, 377-388.

White, B. An experimental approach on the effects of experience on early human behavior. In J. Hill (Ed.), *Minnesota Symposium on Child Psychology*. Minneapolis: University of Minnesota Press, 1967.